THE 2010 PAKISTAN FLOODS ENVIRONMENTAL AND ECONOMIC IMPACT

Tasawwur Husain Zaidi

KNOWLEDGE WORLD
KW Publishers Pvt Ltd
New Delhi

Pakistan Studies Programme
Academy of International Studies
Jamia Millia Islamia
New Delhi

Pakistan Studies Programme
Academy of International Studies
Jamia Millia Islamia
Maulana Mohd. Ali Jauhar Marg
New Delhi 110025

Tel: 91-11-26987582
Telefax: 91-11-26987583
Email: pspjmi@gmail.com
Website: http://www.jmi.ac.in

ISBN 978-93-83649-45-7

Published in India by Kalpana Shukla

KW Publishers Pvt Ltd
4676/21, First Floor, Ansari Road, Daryaganj, New Delhi 110002
+91-11-23263498/43528107 knowledgeworld@vsnl.net www.kwpub.com

2011 FPBA BEST PUBLISHERS AWARD (ENGLISH)

Printed and bound in India

Contents

Acknowledgement

When the 2010 Pakistan floods occurred, I was just completing my Ph.D in Geography. Never in my lifetime, have I had the opportunity to follow such devastating floods. I had just worked on environmental sustainability, economics and society for my doctoral thesis. Therefore, I wanted to understand and analyse why such a devastating flood had taken place, its impact and how the country was coping with it. Given my background, I was encouraged to do a comprehensive analysis of the floods hoping the study will be useful to future generations. There are many lessons to be learnt from these floods. I hope this study will be useful to analysts and policy-makers to put in place proper mechanisms to deal with such floods in the future.

I had the benefit of advice and guidance from many of my teachers to do a truly interdisciplinary study of geology, physiography, hydrology and climate of Pakistan on the one hand and disaster impact assessment, economic aspects, displacement, poverty, deprivation and public response on the other. I am privileged to have been guided by Prof. S.M. Rashid (Department of Geography, JMI), Prof. M.H. Qureshi (A.M. Khwaja Chair, JMI), Prof. M.S. Bhatt (Department of Economics, JMI), and Dr. Ghulam Mohamad Shah (MMAJ, Academy of International Studies, JMI). I express my sincere gratitude to them. This monograph has benefitted from all of them. I shall also remain thankful to my supervisor Prof. Mohammad Firoz Khan for his valuable suggestions and exposing me to conceptual literature on flood-related issues.

Many of my colleagues were very helpful during the course of this study. I am thankful to Mr. Syed Sulaiman Ahmad who guided me in writing the introduction part and also provided me valuable comments at various stages of the completion of this monograph. I am grateful to Dr. Mathew Joseph C. for his overall guidance and editorial assistance. I offer my sincere thanks to Prof. Ajay Darshan Behera, Coordinator of the Programme, for his invaluable advice and guidance and patient editing of several drafts of the monograph.

I would also like to thank my friends Dr. Shahzad Ansari for helping me in cartographic work and Dr. Javed Zafar and Dr. Shahnawaz Khan for their support and encouragement. Finally, I thank my parents and wife Gulnaz Jabi and two beautiful daughters Zaina Zaidi and Airah Zaidi for putting up with my long hours of study to complete this monograph.

Tasawwur Husain Zaidi

New Delhi

1. Introduction

Pakistan came into existence on 14 August 1947 as a result of the partition of British India. It is located between 23°35′ to 37°05′ north latitude and 60°50′ to 77°50′ east longitude, touching the Hindu Kush, Karakoram and Pamir mountains in the north and extending up to the Arabian Sea in the south. It covers an area of 7,82,798 km^2 excluding 13,297 km^2 area of Pakistan Occupied Kashmir (POK) which it had illegally occupied in 1947. In terms of total area, Pakistan is the 36th largest country in the world. It is mainly a sub-tropical country and has a 1,046 kilometre coastline along the Arabian Sea (Figure 1). Pakistan consists of four provinces and four federal territories. With an estimated population of 177.10 million in mid 2011, and an annual growth rate of 2.07 per cent, it is expected that this country may become the fourth largest in terms of the population size by 2050.[1] At present, Pakistan is the world's sixth most populous country with a semi-industrialised economy, mainly dependent on the agriculture sector.[2] A large majority of the population lives in fertile plains of Punjab and Indus River basin.[3] The growth poles of Pakistan's economy are also situated along the Indus River.[4] The fertile tracts of this river have been witnessing rapid land use changes

---

1. Ministry of Finance, Government of Pakistan, *Economic Survey of Pakistan 2010-2011* (Islamabad: Economic Adviser's Wing, Finance Division, Government of Pakistan, 2011), p. 151.
2. S.R. Henneberry, M.E. Khan and K. Piewthongngam, "An Analysis of Industrial–Agricultural Interactions: A Case Study in Pakistan," *Agricultural Economics*, Vol. 22, Issue 1, January 2000, pp. 17-27.
3. Pakistan Bureau of Statistics, Government of Pakistan, *Compendium on Environment Statistics of Pakistan 2010* (Islamabad: Government of Pakistan, 2010), p. 16.
4. Husain Ahmad, *Growth and Dispersion of Manufacturing Industries in Pakistan: A Study in Location and Regionalisation*, Ph.D thesis submitted to the University of Karachi, Pakistan, 1995; World Bank, *Pakistan - Balochistan Economic Report: From Periphery to Core*, Volume II, Report No. 40345-PK, May 2008, p. 2, and A.A. Burki and M.A. Khan, "Spatial Inequality and Geographic Concentration of Manufacturing Industries in Pakistan," Paper presented in *26th Annual General Meeting and Conference 28-30 December 2010* at Pakistan Institute of Development Economics, pp. 1-29. Available at http://pide.org.pk/psde/25/pdf/agm26/day3/Abid%20A.%20Burki.pdf (Accessed on 3 July 2013).

and infrastructure development due to increasing concentration of population, urbanisation and industrial development.

Pakistan suffers from many natural and anthropogenic hazards that threaten the lives and livelihood of its citizens. Natural disasters including floods, earthquakes, landslides, cyclones, drought as well as human-induced disasters such as wars, civil unrest, terrorism, epidemics, accidents and fires are recurrent problems in Pakistan. Since the creation of the country, thousands of people have lost their lives and the properties of billions of dollars have been destroyed due to these hazards. The country has also been impacted by the problem of refugees and internally displaced people (IDPs) who add to the economic burden and many other problems.

Among these disasters, floods are one of the deadliest hazards responsible for thousands of deaths and widespread destruction of properties and resources in almost all parts of Pakistan. For last many years, Pakistan has been repeatedly affected by widespread floods exposing the vulnerability of a large section of its population. The country, which has already been going through many internal problems, the occurrence of natural disasters especially floods have only added to the problems of both the economy and the natural environment which is the very life support system. In a series of natural disasters occurring in this part of South Asia, in 2010, Pakistan faced one of the deadliest floods in its history and the present study tries to analyse the environmental and economic impact of these floods.

The present study is an attempt at a comprehensive understanding of the development, progression, and impact of the floods in Pakistan. Therefore, the first chapter is devoted to a study of those physical aspects of the country which are responsible for the development, movement, modification and severity of the floods. The second chapter is devoted to the study of the floods with a special emphasis on the 2010 floods in Pakistan. This chapter also discusses flood management and response in Pakistan. The third chapter presents a detailed study of the environmental damage/losses and chapter four is dedicated to a comprehensive study of the economic losses. Chapter five analyses the impact of the floods on the environment and different sectors of the economy. The damage and loss discussed in the present study are mainly based on the data provided by the World Health Organisation (WHO), United Nations Office for the Coordination of Humanitarian Affairs (UNOCHA), United Nations Development Programme (UNDP), Food and Agriculture Organisation (FAO), United Nations Human Settlements Programme (UNHSP), World Bank (WB), Asian Development Bank (ADB), National Disaster Management Authority (NDMA), Meteorological Department of the Government of Pakistan, and many other agencies and departments of the Government of Pakistan. Data for damage and need assessment (DNA) has been mainly taken from the "Pakistan Floods 2010: Preliminary Damage and Needs Assessment" prepared by the World Bank and Asian Development Bank with the help of the Government of Pakistan, and, "National Flood Reconstruction Plan 2010" of the Planning Commission, Government of Pakistan.

Methodology and structure of the study of the damage and losses of the present study are based on United Nations Economic Commission for Latin America and the Caribbean (ECLAC) Handbook which describes the methods required for assessing the social, economic and environmental effects of disasters, breaking them down into direct damages and indirect losses and into overall and macroeconomic effects.[5] The term "impact" in the present study means relative changes and resultant implications/problems and opportunities brought in by the occurrence of floods.

Physiography

The study of the geomorphic features of Pakistan is necessary to understand flooding pattern, inundation and carrying out rescue work. Pakistan is a land of many and varying landscapes including mountains, hills, plateaus, plains and deserts. All these features affect and modify water flow. Northern mountains and western plateau cover 58.79 per cent of its area. The remaining 41.21 per cent area comprises a level plain in south and eastern part of the country. The northern and western mountains and highlands are the result of mountain building processes. These mountains are responsible for much of the monsoon

5. Economic Commission for Latin America and the Caribbean (ECLAS), *Handbook for Estimating the Socio-economic and Environmental Effects of Disasters* (Santiago de Chile: ECLAC and World Bank, 2003).

rainfall in Pakistan. The general slope from northern mountains and western plateau is towards south and east. The Indus plains have resulted from the deposition of silts brought by the Indus River and its tributaries into the shallow bays. The general slope in the plain area is from the Himalayan piedmont in the north to the Arabian Sea in the south. The average gradient of the slope is no more than one metre per five kilometres. Except for the micro relief, the plain is featureless. With these characteristics this region with dense concentration of human population is most vulnerable to floods. For the study of the onset of floods, water movements and spatial inundation, Pakistan may be divided into following five physiographic regions (Figure 2).

The Himalayas

The Himalayas are folded mountains located in northern part of the country covering POK and comprise a series of ranges which have great influence on the drainage and climatic conditions of Pakistan. These ranges occurring from south to north include: the Sub-Himalayas or Shiwaliks (600 and 900 metres), the Lesser Himalayas (3,600-4,500 metres), the Great Himalayas (6,000 metres), the Inner Himalayas or Ladakh Range (average height over 3,000 metres) and the Trans-Himalayas or Karakoram Range (average height 6,100 metres). Thus, the average height of these ranges varies between 600 to 6,100 metres from south to north.

These ranges are arranged roughly from southeast to northwest direction. Their horizontal arrangement and altitude present an orographic barrier to the southwest monsoons and is responsible for most of the rainfall in this region. Many glaciers which are located at higher altitude feed several small rivers and streams of the region. The glacial water and heavy monsoon rainfall are responsible for much of flooding in Pakistan. The Sub-Himalayas or Shiwaliks do not have glaciers but they obstruct water movement of the streams coming from higher altitudes. A lot of debris from these hills accumulate near the foothills and plain areas and cause flooding. The mountains of Pakistan are generally affected by flash floods and landslides. A combined effect of deforestation, climate change and some human activities has made mountains of Pakistan more vulnerable to floods and loss of properties and human lives.

The Hindu Kush and the Western Mountains

The Hindu Kush branch off from the Himalayas at the Pamir Knot, where the borders of Pakistan, Afghanistan and China meet. Its direction is roughly from north to south and guards the borders of Pakistan. The Kabul, Swat, Panjkora, and Kunar River flow through these ranges and join the Indus River. From south of the river Kabul up to the Kurram Pass is located the Koh-i-Safed Range (average height 3,600 metres). The Waziristan Hills (1,500-3,000 metres) with east-west direction are located towards the south of these ranges and bounded by the River Gomal. The Sulaiman Mountains (average height 600 metres) are located south of the Gomal River up to the Bugti and Marri Hills. The Kirthar Hills (average height 300 metres) running north-south are located towards the west of the Lower Indus Plain.

Flash floods are one of the most common forms of natural disaster in the Hindu Kush and the western mountains region. This region is particularly vulnerable to this type of flood as a result of the steep slopes, high rate of erosion, and intense seasonal precipitation, particularly during the summer monsoon in the central and eastern Himalayas and in winter in the western Himalayas. Changing watershed and environmental conditions are also increasing this vulnerability.[6]

The Balochistan Plateau

It is a dry area located in the west of the Sulaiman-Kirthar Mountains. The average height of this plateau is about 600 metres. It is covered by hills and mountains with several basins lying between them. The mountain ranges located in the north eastern part of Baluchistan are higher than those of on the western side. This region is true desert and an area of mainly inland drainage and dry lakes locally known as *hamuns.* Important rivers of the Balochistan Plateau include the Zhob Loralai, Hingol, Hab, Porali and Dasht. The four rivers of this region namely Hab, Porali, Hingol and Dasht flow towards south and fall into the Arabian Sea. Along the coast there are large areas of level mud flats forming the coastal plain.

6. A.B. Shrestha, *Managing Flash Flood Risk in the Himalayas,* Information Sheet No. 1/10, (Kathmandu: International Centre for Integrated Mountain Development, ICIMOD, 2010), p.1. Available at http://www.preventionweb.net/files/13252_icimodmanagingflshfloodriskinthehim.pdf (Accessed on 11 August 2013).

The Potwar Plateau and the Salt Range

The average height of the Potwar Plateau is 300-600 metres and covers an area of 18,000 square kilometres. It is bounded by river Jehlum on the east, Indus on the west, Kala Chitta Range and the Margala Hills on the north and the Salt Range on the south. The Soan River and its tributaries have eroded this region and developed several gullies. The Salt Range rises up to an average height of 750-900 metres. The Sakesar (1,527 metres) is the highest peak. The Khabeki, Sakesar and Kallar Kahar are some of the important lakes of this region.

The Indus Plain

The Indus Plain (1,81,299 km^2) is the westward extension of the Indo-Gangetic Plain. This plain has been developed by the deposition laid down by the river Indus and its tributaries. It is divided into three sub-plains: the Upper Indus Plain, the Lower Indus Plain and the South Eastern Desert. The Upper Indus Plain is the land of Jhelum, Chenab, Ravi, Sutlej and Indus rivers, with average height of 120-360 metres. This is almost a plain area with micro-relief. The rivers flowing through this region form meanders and develop flood plain and interfluves. This sub-plain is further divided into four large *doabs* (tracts of land lying between two converging or confluent rivers. It is similar to an interfluve) i.e. the Sindh Sagar Doab or Thal Desert, the Chaj Doab, the Rechna Doab and the Bari Doab.

The Lower Indus Plain or Sindh Plain is almost flat with average gradient of one metre in ten kilometres. This plain is divided into the Kachhi-Sibi Plain, the Sindh Plain and the Indus Delta. The South-Eastern Desert is a dry and hot area with less rainfall. It spreads over an extensive area in eastern Bahawalpur division covering Ghotki, Sukkur, Khairpur, Sanghar, Mirpur Khas and Tharparkar districts. This region is covered with sand dunes rising up to 150 metres. All parts of the Indus Plain are affected by extensive floods and destruction.

Climate

Pakistan is a sub-tropical country characterised by monsoon and continental type of climate. It has four seasons: winter (December to March), summer (April to

June), monsoon or summer rainy (July to September), and autumn or post-monsoon (October to November) season.[7] The average minimum and maximum temperature in winter season during the month of January in the plains of Pakistan has been recorded as 4°C and 24°C respectively. In summer, the minimum temperature during the month of June/July remains around 30°C and maximum temperature increases up to 48°C. The maximum temperature recorded in Sibi and Jacobabad in southern Pakistan has been as high as 52°C. Very high altitude modifies the climate in northern mountainous region; whereas average temperature in the Balochistan Plateau is higher. An analysis of the spatial distribution of average maximum temperature reveals that it decreases from 32-34°C in southern Punjab to 16-20°C in POK. The distribution of average minimum temperature also follows a similar pattern and decreases from 24-26°C in southern Punjab and northern Sindh to 5-12°C in Malakand and Hazara region and 5°C in western Balochistan.

In alignment with global trends, average annual temperature in Pakistan has also increased by 0.6°C during the last century. This increase over northern Pakistan has been higher than that of southern Pakistan (0.8°C versus 0.5°C). Occurence of precipitation over Pakistan has also increased on an average by 25 per cent. Studies based on the ensemble outputs of several Global Circulation Models (GCMs) project that the average temperature over Pakistan may increase in the range 1.3-1.5°C by 2020s, 2.5-2.8°C by 2050s, and 3.9-4.4°C by 2080s, corresponding to an increase in average global surface temperature by 2.8-3.4°C by the turn of the 21st century. Availability of precipitation is projected to increase slightly in summer and decrease in winter with no significant change in annual amount. Furthermore, it is projected that climate change will increase the variability of monsoon rains and enhance the frequency and severity of extreme events such as floods and droughts.[8]

Along the coasts, the climate is modified by sea breezes. In the summer, local hot winds called *loo* (a strong, hot and dry summer afternoon wind from the west) blows across the plains during the daytime. In arid regions relative humidity decreases to 30-35 per cent and trees of the region shed their leaves to avoid loss of moisture. In plain and arid areas the dry and hot weather is occasionally

7. K.U. Kureshy, *Geography of Pakistan* (Lahore: National Book Service Lahore, 1998).
8. Planning Commission, Government of Pakistan, *Task Force on Climate Change, Final Report* (Islamabad: Government of Pakistan, January 2010), p. 2.

broken by the dust and thunderstorms that temporarily lower the temperatures. Evenings in Pakistan are generally cool and the diurnal variation in temperature may be as high as 11 to 17°C. The monsoons (July to September) and the Western Depressions (December to March) are two sources of rainfall in Pakistan. A major part of southern Pakistan is arid to semi-arid and only a small area in the northern part of the country lies in a humid region.[9]

Monsoons are the source of 50 to 75 per cent of summer rainfall in Pakistan. This season normally starts in July and continues till the end of September. During the Monsoon, in most cases, low-pressure area develops in the Bay of Bengal and moves towards Pakistan along the periphery of the Tibetan sub-tropical high (an anticyclone or high pressure formed over the plateau during the summer monsoon period). Sometimes, the low-pressure area also develops in the North Arabian Sea and moves towards Pakistan. However, the Bay of Bengal is more active than the North Arabian Sea with respect to formation of cyclones. In addition, the low-pressure area also develops in the north of Pakistan due to the frontal weather systems that move along the westerly waves over mid-latitudes from west to east during the Monsoon season. According to the climate data for the period of 1960-2009, during the monsoon season, the interaction of westerly and easterly weather systems (developing in the north Arabian Sea, West Asia and the Bay of Bengal) takes place over the north-eastern part of Pakistan and causes heavy rainfall. The duration of such interaction is normally 8 to 12 hours.[10] The distribution of rainfall in Pakistan varies widely. The amount of rainfall decreases from northeast (humid areas) to southwest (arid areas) over the Indus plain.[11]

A spatial analysis of rainfall distribution reveals that it generally decreases from east to west and south to north. A major part of southern Pakistan including parts of Sindh, Baluchistan, Punjab and some areas of Khyber Pakhtunkhwa (KP)

9. F.K. Khan, *Pakistan: Geography, Economy and People* (Karachi: Oxford University Press, 2006), p. 38.
10. World Meteorological Organisation, *WMO Fact Finding and Needs Assessment Mission to Pakistan, Mission Report*, Islamabad: World Meteorological Organization, 4-8 November 2010, pp. 8-9.
11. S.A. Kazi, "Climatic Regions of West Pakistan," *Pakistan Geographical Review*, Vol. 6, No.1, 1951, pp.1-22; S.A. Kazi and M.L. Khan, "Variability of Rainfall and its Bearing on Agriculture in the Arid and Semi-Arid Zones of West Pakistan," *Pakistan Geographical Review*, Vol. 6, No.1, 1951, pp. 40-63; Mubashir L. Khan, "Recent Climate Fluctuation over South Asia and the Indian Ocean," *Pakistan Geographical Review*, Vol. 15, No.2, June 1960, pp.18-37; J.A. Khan, *The Climate of Pakistan* (Karachi: Rehber Publishers, 1993), and Khan, *Pakistan: Geography, Economy and People*, Op. Cit., pp. 34-51.

receive less than 250 mm of rainfall. Northern parts of Punjab and Baluchistan, KP and POK receive 250-500 mm of rainfall. True humid conditions are found only in those areas where rainfall increases to 750 mm in plains and 625 mm in highlands. A region comprising northern Punjab, KP and Federally Administered Tribal Areas (FATA) receives 500-750 mm rainfall. In the north-eastern part of Pakistan lies its humid region which includes northern Rawalpindi, Hazara and Malakand. In this region average annual rainfall exceeds 750 mm see Figure 3.

Drainage and Water Flow

In Pakistan, there are three important river systems: the Indus River System, the Inland Drainage and the Drainage of South Baluchistan (Figure 2). The Indus is 2,900 kilometres long and the most important river of Pakistan. It has a catchment area of 9,70,000 square kilometres of which 26 per cent is in hilly region. It originates in Manasarovar Lake in China and enters in Pakistan at Kalabagh. In Sindh, it forms many channels, meanders, oxbow lakes, levees and deltas. The important right side tributaries of the Indus are Gilgit, Kabul, Kurram and Gomal. The latter three are utilised for irrigation purposes. These tributaries carry lower volume of water which ranges from 0.3 to 3.0 million cubic feet per second. Their catchment area varies from 1,300 to 10,000 square kilometres. The left side tributaries of the Indus are Jhelum, Chenab, Ravi, Beas and Sutlej.

These rivers have low level of flow from November to February and start rising in spring and early summer and are responsible for floods in Punjab and Sindh provinces. The average annual discharge of the Indus at Attock is 92 million acre feet (MAF) and the combined discharge of its tributaries is about 72 MAF.[12] The floodwaters of these rivers take many days even weeks to reach the Arabian Sea. Due to relatively steeper slopes, the flow of these rivers is rapid in north Pakistan. In the plain region floodwater moves at a lower velocity and inundates vast areas for several days (Figure 4). Inland drainage is found in northern parts of southwestern Balochistan between Chagai and Ras Koh Mountains in the north and the Siahan Mountains in the south. It is a dry area and small rivers of the region disappear into sands after flowing for some distances. The rivers of south

12. Khan, *Pakistan: Geography, Economy and People*, Op. Cit., pp. 15-33.

Balochistan (Hab, Porali, Hingol, Dasht, etc.) have developed independent river systems. They originate from the hills of the province and flow into the Arabian Sea.

Except these rivers there are large networks of canals in Pakistan. These canals irrigate a large area in Pakistan and transfer a huge amount of water during floods. The canal system of Pakistan is the largest integrated irrigation network in the world, serving 42 million acres of contiguous cultivated land.[13] There are 12 inter-river (link) canals with discharge capacities ranging from 5,000-22,000 cusecs. These canals play a vital role in the regulation of water in the Indus Basin Irrigation System (IBIS) (Figure 5). The Rasul-Qadirabad-Balloki-Suleimanki (RQBS) and the Trimmu-Sidhnai-Mailsi-Bahawal (TSMB) canal systems were constructed as a sequel to the signing of the Indus Basin Treaty with a purpose to supply irrigation water, from the Western Rivers to the canal systems that were previously fed from the Eastern Rivers whose waters became exclusive property of India. The RQBS system draws its water from the Rasul Barrage, while the TSMB System gets its share from Trimmu Barrage and feeds a number of canals that it crosses between Ravi and Sutlej Rivers. The aggregate designed capacity of link canal system in Pakistan is 4,078 m3/sec or 1,44,000 cusecs.[14]

The irrigation system of Pakistan at present comprises three major reservoirs, 143 large dams (approximately 3.00 MAF of water holding capacity and a height 15 metres and above) and 18 barrages on the main rivers with a total off-take canals capacity of 7,376 cubic metres per second (cumecs) of irrigation supplies. In addition, there are 12 inter-river link canals with a capacity of about 4,076 cumecs which transfer water from surplus to deficient areas. The network now comprises over 56,073 km of irrigation canals, 18,884 km of seepage-cum-storm water drains and 12,612 km of the canals in the Indus Plain. The network of canals includes 45 independent canal commands supplying water to some 4,000 distributaries

13. Husnain Ahmad, Javeed Iqbal Bokhari and Qazi Tallat Mahmood Siddiqui, "Flashflood Risk Assessment in Pakistan," Paper No. 707, in *Pakistan Engineering Congress, 71st Annual Session Proceedings*, 26-30 July 2011 (Lahore: Pakistan Engineering Congress, 2011), pp. 695-708. Available at http://pecongress.org.pk/images/upload/books/FLASHFLOOD%20RISK%20ASSESSMENT%20IN%20PAKISTAN%20 (28).pdf (Accessed on 11 September 2013).

14. Project Management and Policy Implementation Unit (PMPIU), *Handbook on Water Statistics of Pakistan*, (Islamabad: Ministry of Water and Power, Government of Pakistan, 2011), pp. 67-68.

and 1,07,000 watercourses serving 14.6 million hectares (Mha) of canal irrigated land. The total length of main canals/distributaries is 64,000 kilometres while watercourses comprise another 1,621,000 kilometres.[15]

There are two main storage dams on the Indus River System, the Tarbela Dam on the Indus River and Mangla Dam on the Jhelum River, having a combined (current) live storage capacity of 14.42 billion cubic metres (BCM) (11.65 MAF). A third reservoir, Chashma, with a live storage capacity of approximately 0.4 BCM (0.26 MAF), serves primarily as a regulation facility (Table 1). These reservoirs play an important role in regulating natural flows, and releasing of suitable amount of the seasonal water for agriculture and other purposes.

The original combined live storage capacity of Tarbela, Mangla and Chashma reservoirs (14.31 MAF) had reduced to 11.91 MAF in 2011 on account of siltation and mismanagement. Their storage capacity is likely to decline further to 10.0 MAF by the year 2025. As the sedimentation of the reservoir is taking place, it is resulting in progressively reduced regulation capability as well as decreased water availability for irrigation also. During floods, they hold comparatively low amount of water to save down-stream and low lying areas.

Diversion of river waters into main canals is made through barrages which are very helpful in diverting flood water and regulating surface flow. These barrages have been constructed on all major rivers to divert waters in the rivers, link canals and canal commands. The main canals deliver water to branch canals, distributaries and minors. This way water flow is controlled during floods.

15. Water and Power Development Authority (WAPDA), *Annual Reports 2010-11* (Lahore: Ministry of Water & Power, Government of Pakistan, 2011), p. 64. Available a thttp://www.wapda.gov.pk/pdf/Annual%20Report%202010-11.pdf (Accessed on 15 September 2013).

2. Floods in Pakistan

A Brief History of Floods in Pakistan

Since its creation, Pakistan has faced many widespread and devastating floods and almost all regions of Pakistan are vulnerable. At least 27 major floods have hit the country since 1947 and caused great environmental and economic losses of more than US $ 35 billion. After independence, in 1950 a severe flood claimed 2,190 human lives and affected 10,000 villages. As far as loss of human lives is concerned, this was the greatest loss in the recorded history of floods in Pakistan. In 1956, widespread floods covering 74,406 square kilometre area and 11,609 villages caused great loss of properties and claimed around 160 human lives (Table 2).

After the war of 1971 and resultant division of Pakistan, the economy of the country was undergoing difficulties and the flood of 1973 with a monetary loss of more than US $ 5 billion further complicated the recovery and development process. Again in 1976, one of the most widespread and devastating flood caused a loss of about US $ 3.5 billion. In 1977, at least 848 persons lost their lives due to floods. In 1978, a major flood claimed 393 lives with a monetary loss of more than US $ 2.2 billion. Thus, during the 1970s at least 2,266 persons lost their lives and a monetary loss of around US $ 12 billion also occurred. All these figures indicate vulnerability of people to flood hazards (Table 2). Therefore, Pakistan has become one of the five South Asian countries with the highest annual average number of people physically exposed to floods.[16]

According to recorded data for the decade of the1980s, floods hazards claimed 641 lives and caused a monetary loss of more than US $ 1.3 billion. A major flood

16. World Conference on Disaster Reduction (WCDR), *A Review of Disaster Management Policies and Systems in Pakistan* (Islamabad, 2005), p. 5. Available at http://saarc-sdmc.nic.in/pdf/pakistan/file3.pdf (Accessed on 16 September 2013).

struck the country in 2003 and devastated many properties resulting in a loss of more than US $ 5 billion. Between 2001 and 2007 more than 1,950 persons lost their lives. Except properties and lives, the loss to environment by floods has been far more incalculable. Pakistan had barely recovered from the destruction of the 2005 earthquake when in 2010 it was worst hit by deadly and widespread floods which left the country even more vulnerable to future floods and other hazards (Table 2). In recent years, rising incidence of loss of life and property also indicates relative un-preparedness of governments and their institutions to deal with such hazards.

Causes of Floods in Pakistan

There are many hydro-meteorological, anthropogenic and geomorphologic causes of floods in Pakistan. Some of them include heavy and concentrated rainfall in the river catchments augmented by snowmelt flows; siltation and obstructions, levees burst and spillover, surface gradient, river basin shape and size, etc. (Figure 6). In the upper part of the Indus, floodwater spilling over the riverbanks generally returns to the river. However, in its lower part in Sindh it generally flows at a higher elevation than adjoining lands, the spill flows do not return to the river and cause floods and damages. Breaches of river embankments often cause greater damage than would have occurred without the bunds because of their unexpected nature and intensification of land use. The inadequate existing discharge capacity of some of the important structures (barrages and rail or road bridges) on the Indus, Chenab and Ravi is also one of the major reasons for flooding.

The encroachment of settlements in riverine areas has also increased the quantum of flood damages and losses to humans and livestock. As there is no proper regulatory frame work in the country regarding the settlement in riverine areas, most of the landless poor people have constructed their shelters along the vulnerable river banks and become victims to devastating floods. Due to encroachment and unplanned use of river catchments in recent years, vulnerabilities of large cities to flooding have increased. Cities like Karachi, Lahore and Rawalpindi have experienced flooding due to improper land utilisation and drainage system. This problem is likely to be more serious in the coming years due to increasing population and unplanned settlements along rivers and water channels.

Climate Change and global warming are also being held responsible as major drivers of floods. According to the experts from World Climate Research Programme (WCRP) and the World Meteorological Organisation (WMO), climate change has been a major contributing factor in "unprecedented sequence of extreme weather in Pakistan" in months of July and August 2010. Intergovernmental Panel on Climate Change (IPCC) also warns: "the floods of the kind that hit Pakistan in 2010 may become more frequent and more intense in the future in the same region and other parts of the world."[17] Earlier, the WMO made a similarly qualified assessment that the weather related cataclysms of July and August (2010) fit patterns predicted by climate scientists. They also stated: "While a longer time range is required to establish whether an individual event is attributable to climate change, the sequence of current events matches IPCC projections of more frequent and more intense extreme weather events due to global warming."[18]

On the contrary, recently many scientists have concluded that climate change is not a major cause of floods; instead they have suggested anthropogenic and geomorphologic causes being more responsible for widespread damages.[19] The Flood Inquiry Commission appointed by the Supreme Court of Pakistan has also blamed anthropogenic causes including negligence and corruption to be responsible for floods in many parts of the country. Several other studies have also derived same results about the 2010 floods in Pakistan.[20]

17. Hashim Nisar Hashmi, Qazi Tallat Mahmood Siddiqui, Abdul Razzaq Ghumman, Mumtaz Ahmed Kamal and Habib ur Rehman Mughal, "A Critical Analysis of 2010 Floods in Pakistan," *African Journal of Agricultural Research*, Vol. 7, No. 7, 19 February 2012, pp. 1054-67.
18. Federal Flood Commission, Government of Pakistan, *Annual Flood Report 2010* (Islamabad: Ministry of Water and Power, Government of Pakistan, 2010), p. 10. Available at http://www.ffc.gov.pk/download/flood/archieve/Annual.report2010.pdf (Accessed on 22 July 2013).
19. J. Edgar, "Climate Change not Main Cause of Floods, Scientists Suggest," *The Telegraph*, 22 January 2014. Available at http://www.telegraph.co.uk/earth/environment/10588783/Climate-change-not-main-cause-of-floods-scientists-suggest.html (Accessed on 24 January 2014).
20. M.A. Khan, F.K. Khan, A.W. Kazi, K.Z. Ahmed, Report of the Flood Inquiry Commission, Appointed by the Supreme Court of Pakistan (Supreme Court of Pakistan, 2011). Available at http://www.pakissan.com/english/watercrisis/flood/report.of.flood.inquiry.commission.shtml (Accessed on 23 September 2013); P.J. Webster, V. E. Toma, and H. M. Kim, "Were the 2010 Pakistan Floods Predictable?" *Geophysical Research Letters*, Vol. 38, Issue 4, February 2011, pp. 1-5, and J.P.M. Syvitski and G. Robert Brakenridge, "Causation and Avoidance of Catastrophic Flooding along the Indus River, Pakistan," *GSA Today* (Washington), Vol. 23, Issue 1, January 2013, pp. 4-10.

The 2010 Floods in Pakistan

The 2010 monsoon brought with it the worst flooding in the past 80 years in Pakistan due to interaction of monsoon winds and mid-latitude westerlies (south westerly belts of winds moving pole-ward in winter and equator-ward in summer). These floods inundated almost 20 per cent area of the country (Figure 7). In 2009, the monsoon system in the country was predominantly affected by the El Niño[21] with rainfall measuring below 26 per cent of normal. The monsoon season in 2010 also started normally until middle of July when northern parts of the country received heavy rainfall in many parts. According to World Meteorological Organization (WMO) fact-finding and needs-assessment mission to Pakistan, in July 2010, the Arabian Sub-Tropical High and Tibetan Sub-Tropical High shifted to north, thus, monsoon weather system which developed on 24 July in the Bay of Bengal moved westward and reached Pakistan on 27 July. This system merged with the seasonal low (already present over Pakistan) and interacted with the westerly wave over north-western part of Pakistan (instead of north-eastern part). The westerly wave was associated with a jet stream of strong wind of more than 100 knots (185 km/h) at 200 millibar. This interaction of two weather systems helped transport the moisture even above 500 millibar levels from the North Arabian Sea and created a thick layer of moist air above the mid-troposphere level over the catchments of Kabul and Indus Rivers. The northward shift of Tibetan Sub-Tropical High acted as a block and caused the interaction to prolong for 36-48 hours and produced extreme rainfall over north-western Pakistan from 28 to 30 July. During this rain spell, the total rainfall in northwest Pakistan amounted to more than 300 mm. From 5 to 9 August 2010, there was another rain spell, again due to interaction of westerly wave and monsoon weather system of a lesser intensity. This interaction caused

21. El Niño is an unusual interaction between air and sea in the equatorial Pacific and may be defined as an invasion of warm surface water from the western part of the equatorial Pacific into the normally cooler waters of the central and eastern part of the Pacific Basin off the western coast of South America – mainly Peru and Ecuador. El Niño events are marked by a weakening of the easterly surface winds, as well as the east–west gradients in sea level and thermocline depth. These events have great impact on the Indian monsoon system generally characterised by very low availability of rainfall in the region. For detail see John E. Oliver, *Encyclopedia of World Climatology* (Dordrecht, The Netherlands: Springer, 2005), pp. 349-51.

widespread rains in Pakistan especially heavy rainfall was received in northern and central parts of the country.[22] Many places in KP, POK and Punjab received heavy rainfall of more than 200 mm (Table 3).

The first heavy rain spell (28 to 30 July 2010) in northern Pakistan especially in KP and adjoining upper parts of Punjab caused severe flash flooding followed by extreme riverine flooding. The second rainfall spell (5 to 9 August 2010) generated a second flood wave in the Indus River and its tributaries aggravating the already flooded fields of Punjab, KP and Sindh. This wave practically merged with the first flood wave below Taunsa barrage (on the Indus River in Punjab) and created havoc in the surrounding and downstream areas. Several areas in KP, Baluchistan, Punjab and Sindh were severely affected.[23]

Finally, an interrupted and long spell of intense rainfall in northern and central parts of Pakistan led to devastating floods in many parts of the country. In addition, the torrential rains in Dera Ghazi Khan and Dera Ismail Khan flooded and damaged the surrounding areas. On July 22, 2010, heavy rainfall in Balochistan caused breaching at Lehri Flood Protection Bund and flood water outburst 43 km upstream of Sibi inundating more than 20 villages along its banks. During these floods, flows in western rivers were very high and comparable to those recorded during the floods of 1956, 1976, and 1992.[24] A comparison of historic maximum flood peaks versus 2010 flood maximum flood peaks is given in Table 4. According to this data new records of water level were made at Tarbela, Chashma, and Taunsa dam of the Indus River. Warsak dam of the Kabul River also recorded a historic high of 1,52,710 cusec on 30 July 2010. At other dams and barrages also, huge volumes of water were recorded due to floods and heavy rainfall.

22. World Meteorological Organisation, Op. Cit., pp. 8-9, and Space and Upper Atmosphere Research Commission (SUPARCO) & Food and Agriculture Organization (FAO), *Pakistan Floods/Rains 2010: Rapid Crop Damage Assessment, Series No.1, 30 September 2010* (Karachi: SUPARCO, 2010), p. 1. Available at http://www.suparco.gov.pk/downloadables/PAKISTAN_FLOODRAIN.pdf (Accessed on 22 September 2013).
23. Ibid., pp. 8-9.
24. SUPARCO & FAO, Op. Cit., pp. 1-8.

Spatio-Temporal Analysis of Flooding Patterns

In the following section a detailed spatial and temporal analysis of rainfall, floods and water movements has been carried out to systematically understand the impact of these floods. An understanding of these spatial and temporal events reveals that the heavy rainfall in northern Pakistan caused immense damage and loss of life in southern parts of the country. Space and Upper Atmosphere Research Commission (SUPARCO), the national space agency of Pakistan, utilised the satellite data to develop temporal information for inundation and recession of water from the affected areas (Figure 7). According to this data the first heavy monsoon rainfall was received between 18 to 24 July. The cumulative rainfall during this period was of the order of 1,716 mm. The maximum rainfall of 179 mm was recorded at Mianwali on 22 July 2010. Other areas receiving heavy rains during this period were Abbotabad, Bannu, Muzaffarabad, Faisalabad, Gujranwala, Murree and others. The Swat, Kabul and Indus rivers had received large volumes of water and started rising and overflowing. As a result, flooding in Mianwali (POK) and Layyah (Punjab) districts occurred during this period.[25]

Between 28 and 30 July, the cumulative rainfall of 1,944 mm was observed with maximum of 312 mm being recorded in Peshawar on 29 July. Other areas receiving heavy rainfall during this period were Abbotabad, Chitral, Islamabad, Jhelum, Murree, Muzaffarabad, Rawalpindi, Sialkot, and Karachi. Outflows from Swat and Kabul rivers had affected Swat valley and Charsada/Nowshera districts. The Indus River had flooded many areas in Mianwali, Layyah, D.G. Khan and Rajanpur districts. There was recorded continuous rains for eight days between 2 to 9 August in the catchment areas of the rivers mainly in northern and central parts of Pakistan. The cumulative rainfall during this period was 2,518 mm with maximum of 134 mm being recorded on 7 August at Larkana. These rains set in motion unprecedented floods in Pakistan's history. In Southern Punjab, many breaches in the Indus River had taken place on 2 August at Mullanwala and Dibwala villages upstream the Taunsa barrage. These breaches had caused a wave of 3 to 4 metre high, hitting Daira Din Panah, Kot Addu, Rangpur and other rural areas in Muzaffargarh district.

25. Ibid., pp. 1-11.

On 4 August 2010, the river flow was at 474 thousand cusecs at Kalabagh dam and on 5 August it was around 700 cusecs at Gaddu due to the merger of Chenab River into Indus River at the juncture of Mithankot (Figure 4 & 5). The peak discharge during that period was recorded on 8 August which was 562 thousand cusecs at Kalabagh; 1,149 thousand cusecs at Gaddu and 1,075 thousand cusecs at Sukkur. The flood had not reached Kotri by that time, therefore, the discharge rate was measured as 169 thousand cusecs at this river inflow measurement (RIM) station. The main events of that period were (a) breaches in Indus River and upstream Taunsa barrage, setting a high wave of floods in Muzaffargarh district (b) peak flood in the Indus River extending beyond Sukkur barrage, and (c) flooding of the Katcho areas in upper Sindh.[26]

The cumulative rainfall between 10 and 20 August was 1,072 mm; with a maximum of 75 mm at Islamabad on 20 August. The peak flow of 625 thousand cusecs at Kalabagh was recorded on 10 August. The flood water started receding thereafter at this RIM station and was measured at 452 thousand cusecs on 17 August. At Gaddu, the peak discharge of 1,077 thousand cusecs was noted on 17 August. At Sukkur Barrage two peaks were recorded: first on 12 August with a discharge of 1,132 thousand cusecs and the second one on 17 August with a discharge of 1,026 thousand cusecs. At Kotri Barrage, the water discharge was 188 thousand cusecs on 9 August. It started rising rapidly thereafter and touched 614 thousand cusecs on 20 August. Thus, the consequences of that discharge were, (a) floods touching a peak in Punjab; (b) breaches in embankments of Indus River at Tori and Ghauspur exposing vast fertile agricultural tracts between the river and Kirthar range in Baluchistan and Sindh to inundation, and (c) the rice crop of this area which is predominant cash/food crop was destroyed.

The cumulative rainfall between 21 August and 16 September 2010 was recorded as high as 2,026 mm with a maximum of 113 mm at D.I. Khan on 25 August. The Indus River had already normalised at Kalabagh in Punjab. Consequently, the river flows started falling at Gaddu and Sukkur barrages also. However, at Kotri flood water was still surging. The peak discharge of 965 thousand cusecs at this RIM station was recorded on 27 August. The water entered the deltaic region

26. Ibid., pp. 8-9.

destroying crops and infrastructure. By the end of August 2010, KP and Punjab were cleared of the flood water except some localised low-lying pockets. In Sindh, the flood water continued receding from the flooded areas to the Dadu district. The deltaic region in Thatta district which is predominantly a rice growing area was still inundated. Between 10 to 30 September large areas in flood affected Sindh and some areas in Jaffarabad, Baluchistan remained under deep water and unavailable for sowing *rabi* crops (sown in April-June and harvested in October-December). The *kharif* crops (sown in October-December and harvested in April-May), mainly rice, were already destroyed in this area.[27]

According to data provided by the NDMA and SUPARCO at least 75,633 km^2 or 9.5 per cent area of the country was affected by the floods. The province of Sindh with 28,036 km^2 or 19.90 per cent of its area had been worst affected followed by Punjab (14.35 per cent), KP (12.30 per cent) and Baluchistan (2.35 per cent). As far as total affected area is concerned, Punjab with 29,463 km^2 had suffered widespread floods. As far as duration of flooding was concerned, water remained stagnant in many parts of Sindh for more than two months. It had completely paralysed normal life in the flood-affected areas. A spatial analysis of the severity of floods reveals that 27 districts (mostly along Indus River basin) in Pakistan were severely affected. In each of these districts more than 1,00,000 persons were affected by the floods. Less than 1,00,000 persons were affected by floods in moderately affected 36 districts of the country. In all 78 districts recorded various levels of flooding. Two districts in POK and six districts in GB also suffered from severe floods (Table 5 & Figure 8).

Flood Management and Response

In Pakistan, the multi-functional task of flood management is carried out by a number of organisations of both national as well as provincial government. The government organisations responsible for flood management are the Provincial Irrigation Departments (PIDs), Pakistan Water and Power Development Authority (WAPDA), Provincial Relief Organisations, Pakistan Army, Pakistan Commissioner for Indus Waters (PCIW), Emergency Relief Cell (ERC) of the Cabinet Division,

27. Ibid., pp. 9-10.

Federal Flood Commission (FFC), Flood Forecasting Division (FFD) and National Disaster Management Authority (NDMA), Provincial Disaster Management Authorities (PDMAs) and the District Administration.

Till 1976, the provincial governments were responsible for the planning and execution of flood protection measures. With the establishment of FFC in 1977, they took the responsibility for integrated planning for flood control at the national level and arranging financial resources for the implementation of flood management projects on a countrywide basis. Since its establishment, FFC has so far prepared and executed three National Flood Protection Plans (NFPP) covering periods from 1978-88 (NFPP-I), 1988-98 (NFPP-II) and 1998-2008 (NFPP-III). The NFPP-IV (2008-18) was under approval by the Planning Commission, while flood protection measures are being undertaken through Normal/Emergent Flood Programme on yearly basis to meet urgent need of the Provinces and Federal Line Agencies. The NDMA established in 2006 serves as the focal point and coordinates to facilitate implementation of disaster risk management strategies.[28]

As far as Pakistan's response to disasters is concerned, it had been 'response centric' till 2005 when the country faced a massive earthquake and lost thousands of people and properties worth billions of dollar. The continuous onslaught of disasters compelled Pakistan to move towards a 'preparedness and prevention approach' thus bringing about a paradigm shift in its overall Disaster Risk Management (DRM) agenda. The Government of Pakistan also passed the National Disaster Management Act, 2010 which includes preparedness, response, recovery and rehabilitation, and reconstruction under the meaning of disaster management.

The Federal Flood Commission has also prepared a road map for a comprehensive flood management plan. The commission has also been advised to prepare district/area-wise comprehensive flood fighting plan by the provinces/federal line agencies depending upon the vulnerability of the area. Many engineering projects have also been started by the federal and provincial governments. Effective arrangements have been made for liaison with Flood Forecasting Division (FFD) Lahore, Meteorological Department of Pakistan and the WAPDA for issuance of flood warnings well in time upto the levels of district administration. Recently more

28. Federal Flood Commission, Op. Cit., pp. 4-18.

emphasis is being laid on implementation of plans by increasing coordination and updating of information.[29]

During the floods of 2010, The Government of Pakistan (including provincial governments) launched rescue and relief operations. The NDMA in collaboration with the UN and other development partners prepared a Strategic Early Recovery Action Plan (SERAP) covering eight key sectors (agriculture and food security, health and nutrition, water and sanitation, education, housing, governance, non-farm livelihoods (NFL), community physical infrastructure and addressed four cross-cutting themes: protection, gender, the environment and disaster risk reduction.[30] To provide ready cash to the flood-affected population, the Government of Pakistan in collaboration with National Database and Registration Authority (NADRA) distributed 9,77,570 Watan Cards (US $ 235.30 per family) throughout the country.[31]

The Pakistan military also helped during the floods and later recovery and rehabilitation efforts. The international community also offered financial and technical assistance to the Government. Pledges from sixty-eight bilateral and multilateral donors totaling US $ 1,870.2 million in the form of grants and in-kind contributions, were committed to the Government for the relief and early recovery phases. But, even after the recession of the floods, Pakistan received only US $ 489.5 million, of which US $ 202 million was in kind, which had gone into meeting humanitarian and emergency relief needs. A broad range of international and national NGOs worked with the Government to provide emergency relief support to the affected populations throughout the country. The private sector (individuals, corporations and foundations) contributed over US $ 17 million to the flood relief effort, with the majority of the funds passed on to various UN organisations and NGOs.[32]

---

29. Ibid., p. 13-14.
30. National Disaster Management Authority (NDMA), Government of Pakistan & United Nations Development Programme (UNDP), *Early Recovery-Floods 2010,* Final Report, March 2012, (Islamabad: United National Development Programme, 2012), p. 11. Available at http://pdma.gov.pk/downloads/Early%20Recovery%20Report%20-%20Flood%202010.pdf (Accessed on 11 November 2013).
31. World Bank, Asian Development Bank & Government of Pakistan, *Pakistan Floods 2010: Preliminary Damage and Needs Assessment* (Islamabad: 2010), p. 20. Available at https://www.gfdrr.org/sites/gfdrr.org/files/publication/Pakistan_DNA.pdf (Accessed on 27 July 2013).
32. Ibid., p. 20.

3. Environmental Damage and Losses Due to the 2010 Floods

The 2010 floods had resulted in huge environmental damage and heightened risks. The capacity of flood water to damage is determined by the volume, velocity and duration of flood waters. Suspended particles and rocks carried by floodwater act as tools of erosion and damage. Intensity and volume of precipitation determine velocity, area coverage and stagnation period. Likewise, habitats, diversity and density of fauna and flora; topography and soil characteristics of the flood area determine environmental impact. Therefore, the geographical, geological and cultural features of an area are major determinants of the intensity of floods and their impacts. Floods affect both, physical environment and cultural environment (infrastructure, humans and their livelihood) which generally leads to the loss of environmental health and services (Table 6).

As far as environmental impact of floods is concerned, it is not always negative. It has many positive impacts also like soil development, water recharge, environmental cleaning, etc. In the present study the meaning of environmental impact is not confined to direct loss or degradation of the environment but it includes indirect impact on cultural environment also (Figure 9). Heavy and continuous rainfall in many parts of Pakistan resulted in huge volumes of water which spread to cause widespread flooding and stagnation. In many areas of Punjab, Sindh and Balochistan it took more than two months for these floods to recede and affected every area including mountains, forests, wetlands and other natural systems.

As far as damage and loss of flora and fauna is concerned, an estimated 80 per cent of reptile and small mammal habitats were affected within the Swat and Panjorka river catchments. According to FAO estimates, 1.2 million heads of livestock were lost, which does not include the 6 million poultry (72 per cent of pre-floods stock) lost. The flood damage to riparian and non-riparian forests, as well as wildlife resources, as reported by the provinces was estimated at US $ 11.67 million. Loss of riparian vegetation has left river courses more vulnerable to floods in coming years. No detailed studies and estimates are available for the damage to wetlands and mangroves.[33] According to one estimate around 20 per cent of tree plantations developed in 2009-10 were ruined leaving hill slopes susceptible to erosion, reducing interception of rainfall and increasing the intensity of future floods.[34]

According to a rapid assessment, in Swat and Dir, the flood had damaged about 30 to 40 per cent of the 800 acre plantation in Timargarah, about 25 to 35 per cent of the 600 acres plantations in Chakdarra, and about 25 to 35 per cent of the 400 acres plantation in Samar Bagh. The damage to farm forestry near to the river Swat and its tributaries was reported to be ranging from 50 to 80 per cent. According to initial estimates, 30 per cent of the natural forests of Upper Dir District sustained damages either from river overflows, floods, cloud bursts and landslides. In areas along the Jindi, Khayali, and Sardaryab Rivers in Charsadda district, the flood had washed 80 per cent linear plantation, while in areas away from the rivers the damage ranged between 10-20 per cent. In Kund Park (Nowshera district) and in the nearby villages about 50 per cent of trees were uprooted by the flood.[35]

In Muzzafar Garh district, floods had damaged about 45,000 acres or 75 per cent area of communal Bela forests[36], around 315 acres or 25 per cent of canals side linear plantations and uprooted about 20 per cent of the trees of the 380 acres of linear plantations along roads. In Dera Ghazi Khan, floods damaged about 3,000

33. Ibid., p. 33.

34. A. Khan, Khan M. Ayaz, A. Said, Z. Ali, H. Khan, N. Ahmad and R. Garstang, *Rapid Assessment of Flood Impact on the Environment in Selected Affected Areas of Pakistan* (Islamabad: Pakistan Wetlands Programme and UNDP, 2010), p. 3. Available at http://floods2010.pakresponse.info/LinkClick.aspx?fileticket=5MHAZOUGSKQ%3D&tabid=86&mid=548 (Accessed on 13 December 2013).

35. Ibid., pp. 4-5 & pp. 13-14

36 In Pakistan, communal forest is a sub-category of the *Guzara* forest, where entire village owns the forest. The proper management of such lands through participatory and joint forest management techniques is capable of ensuring the economic, ecological, and social benefits to the people. For more details see Mirza B. Baig, Shabbir Ahmad, Nowshad Khan, Imtiaz Ahmad and Gary S. Straquadine, "The History of Social Forestry in Pakistan: An Overview" *International Journal of Social Forestry*, Vol. 1, No., 2, December 2008, pp.167-183. Available at http://www.ijsf.org/dat/art/vol01/ijsf_vol1_no2_04_baig_pakistan.pdf (Accessed on 22 December 2013).

acres of irrigated plantation, while the total forest area damaged was about 25 per cent of the total of 64,000 acres. In this district the damages to the road side linear plantations was about 25 per cent of the total. In Gilgit Baltistan, the floods had destroyed about 9 per cent of the social forestry areas and 8 per cent of the popular block plantations raised for commercial purposes. In this district, floods had also damaged about 16 per cent of the farm forests raised for domestic consumption, 3 per cent of the linear plantations raised along the agricultural fields, about 5 per cent of the linear plantations along the roadsides, and about 4 per cent of the linear plantation along water channels. The biggest damage of about 26 per cent was recorded in Kargah for the plantations along the water channels.[37]

According to the Upper Dir Wildlife Division of the Khyber Pukhtunkhwa Wildlife Department, the damages to *markhor*, a large species of wild goat (*Capra falconeri*) population was about 5 per cent, while about 15 per cent of its habitat was damaged. The flood affected about 15 per cent of the *koklass* pheasants (*Pucrasia macrolopha*) population and about 30 per cent of their habitat. These floods had also destroyed 30 per cent food resources of these pheasants. Total damages assessed for *monal* pheasants (*Lophophorus impejanus*) were about 10 per cent of their population, 30 per cent of their habitat and about 30 per cent of their food resources in the Upper Dir district. According to reports from the local community to the Wildlife Department, mortality of birds in Tangi and Adenzai Community Game Reserves was as much as 50 per cent, their habitat and food resources were also damaged to a similar extent.[38]

In Charsadda and Nowshera districts (KP), the floods resulted in killing 219 wild animals including 37 spotted deer, six hog deer, four *chinkara* deer (*Gazella bennettii*), 28 black bucks, two common leopards, two *urial* sheeps (*Ovis orientalis*), and pheasants that included 21 blue Java peacocks, 19 white peacocks, eight black shouldered peacocks, five silver peasants, and 23 ring-necked pheasants. The flood had damaged the Kund Bear Centre (located in the Kund Park) and killed 20 bears out of total 23 living there. This is the only facility in the country where rescued bears are kept for their rehabilitation. The Taunsa Wildlife Sanctuary covers over 19,625 acres, out of this about 7,500 acres was reserved as the habitat of around

37. Ibid., p.17 & p. 24.
38. All figures cited from Ibid., pp. 5-7.

900 hog deer. According to information from the Punjab Wildlife Department, the floods had affected approximately 25 per cent of the hog deer population. The Indus River is home to the endangered endemic Indus dolphin (*Platanista minor*). Its habitat was also disturbed by floods. The floods also affected about 40-50 per cent of the habitat of wild boar in the districts of central and southern Punjab.[39]

In northern and western parts of the country significant damage was done to fertile soils also especially in areas with steeper slopes and along water courses. Due to steep slope and heavy downpour a great loss of soil was recorded in the Kohistan, Shangla, Lower and Upper Dir, Swat, Nowshera, D. I. Khan and Charsadda districts of KP, Muzaffarabad in POK, Mianwali, D. G. Khan and Rajanpur in Punjab, Nasirabad, Jaffarabad and Kharan in Balochistan and Larkana, Kamber-Shahdadkot, Dadu and Thatta in Sindh. These soils supported different species and varieties of trees and grasses. This vegetation cover in turn provided many ecological and economic benefits including natural beauty.

The loss of soil is difficult to calculate in monetary terms but its importance may be understood by the fact that a small layer of it takes decades or even hundreds of years for its formation. In 2006, the estimated economic losses from reduced yields resulting from soil erosion in Pakistan were around US $ 0.25 billion per year, or 0.25 per cent of the GDP. Offsite costs such as the siltation of dams and changes in hydrology are not included in this figure.[40] In eastern and southern parts vast areas remained submerged for many weeks. In many areas new soil was deposited and erosion took place mainly along water courses.

There are reports of water being contaminated in widespread areas rendering it unsuitable for any consumption by humans. Municipal solid waste generation in the affected communities was estimated at 2,900 tons per day. In the absence of proper cleaning and management that waste got mixed with flood water and contaminated large volumes. Around 62,000 litres of petroleum and 44,300 litres diesel also got released into the flood water from pumps in various parts of

39. Ibid., p. 14 & p. 17.
40. H.D. Foth, *Fundamentals of Soil Science,* 8th Edition (New York: John Wiley & Sons, 1990), p. 252, and World Bank, *Pakistan Strategic Country Environmental Assessment, Vol. 1* (Islamabad: South Asia Environment and Social Development Unit, South Asia Region, 2006), p. 17. Available at http://siteresources.worldbank.org/SOUTHASIAEXT/Resources/Publications/448813-1188777211460/pakceavolume1.pdf (Accessed on 11 August 2013).

Pakistan. It greatly harmed the fauna and flora in the country. Contamination of drinking water, proliferation of disease vectors caused by the stagnation of water and accumulation of pollutants badly affected the health of population, particularly women and children.[41]

According to government reports, 1,961 people lost their lives and 2,907 were injured (Punjab 110 dead and 262 injured; Sindh 293 dead and 1,202 injured; KP 1,156 dead and 1,198 injured; Balochistan 48 dead and 98 injured; POK 71 dead and 87 injured; and GB 183 dead and 60 injured) as a result of the floods. That calamity had marooned around 20 million people and over 1.87 million houses were destroyed. Pakistan suffers an annual loss of 8.84 per cent of its GDP from environmental related diseases. Almost half of this cost is caused by mortality (4.13 per cent of GDP) while the rest (4.71 per cent of GDP) stems from malnutrition caused by environmentally-related diseases. Pakistan's floods of 2010 have further aggravated these problems in the country.[42] The country had also lost thousands of animals, birds and their habitats. In the present study their losses have been explained in the section on damage and losses incurred to agriculture, livestock and fisheries.

Short term or immediate requirements for the recovery and reconstruction of environmental damage were estimated around US $ 209 million. It includes the costs of institutional frameworks, planning, and capacity-building to reduce the risk of floods (US $ 26.30 million); strengthening legal and institutional frameworks (US $ 5.60 million); restoration of natural systems in the Indus watershed (US $ 117.56 million); burden on environmental health and proposed responses (US $ 64.59 million) and additional studies with an amount of US $ 0.40 million. Medium and long-term requirements were set much higher at (US $ 1,864.84 million). It included the costs of forest restoration (US $ 1,326.47 million), riparian vegetation restoration (US $ 280.96 million), wetland restoration (US $ 108.00 million) and mangrove restoration with an amount of US $ 149.41 million (Table 6). In medium and long-term all emphasis has been laid on forests and ecological development to create much needed resilience in the environmental system.

41. WB, ADB & Government of Pakistan, Op. Cit., p. 63.
42. Ibid., p. 63.

4. Economic Damage and Losses Due to the 2010 Floods

According to the damage and need analysis (DNA) prepared by the World Bank and Asian Development Bank with the help of Government of Pakistan, with respect to economic loss and financial costs, the DNA was carried out against three assessment categories where direct damage refers to the monetary value of the completely or partially destroyed assets, such as social, physical and economic infrastructure immediately following a disaster. Wherever possible, the direct damage for assets was assessed at their book values. Indirect losses are income losses, and included both the change of flow of goods and services and other economic flows such as increased expenses, curtailed production and diminished revenue, which arise from the direct damage to production capacity and social and economic infrastructure. Reconstruction costs denote the cost of rebuilding lost assets and restoring lost services. It is generally assessed as the replacement cost with a premium added for building back smarter.

For the measurement of total damage, the whole economy has been divided into different sectors. These sectors have been grouped into four categories: (i) Social infrastructure: housing, health, education; (ii) Physical infrastructure: irrigation and flood management, transport and communications, water supply and sanitation and energy, (iii) Economic sector: agriculture, live stock and fisheries, private sector and industries, financial sector and social protection & livelihood, and (iv) Cross-cutting sector: governance, environment and disaster risk management.[43] A detailed study of the environmental damage/loss and impact has been separately carried out. What follows is a detailed analysis of the economic damage or loss in the different sectors of the economy. Simultaneously, monetary

43. Ibid., p. 14.

need assessment has also been included in the analysis to understand the total losses and their impact on the economy.

The devastating floods of 2010 affected every province, area and sector of the economy of Pakistan. Therefore, for a comprehensive understanding and estimation of the losses/damages, a province-wise analysis has been made to exactly locate and explain the damages (Tables 7 & 8). As far as provincial distribution of total damage/losses is concerned, with 44 per cent of total (direct and indirect) damages, Sindh has been the worst affected followed by Punjab (26 per cent) and the KP (12 per cent). The losses to the federal government accounted for 11 per cent of the total, although most of them consist of indirect losses (US $ 827 million or 75.73 per cent of the total) of federally owned commercial banks and financial institutions. The Government of Pakistan with the WB and ADB estimated total reconstruction cost across the range of three options with option one as the base case and option three as the recommended one. The reconstruction cost for the base case was estimated at US $ 6.799 billion while the recommended option cost was estimated at US $ 8.915 billion (Table 8).

According to some estimates, overall damage had been placed at US $ 10,056 million (with direct losses as US $ 6,496 million and indirect losses US $ 3,560 million) amounting to 5.8 per cent of the GDP for the year 2009-10 (Table 8). Total damage in agriculture sector was recorded to be the highest amounting to US $ 5,045 million or 35.68 per cent of total value of agriculture output at factor cost in 2009-10.[44] Likewise, estimates of damage to the housing sector (US $ 1,588 million) were less than one-third of that of agriculture, yet consisted of almost 39 per cent of the total value of this sector. Transport and communication sector suffered a total loss of US $ 1,328 million amounting to 65.58 per cent of total losses of that sector. Financial sector was mainly indirectly affected with a total loss of US $ 674 million. Education, energy, private sector and industries, irrigation and flood management and water supply and sanitation were other sectors which lost more than US $ 100 million. Each of the other sectors of the economy lost less than US $ 100 million. No estimates of direct and indirect losses are available for social protection & livelihood and disaster risk management. A detailed discussion of the sector-wise immediate losses follows.

44. Pakistan Bureau of Statistics, *Agricultural Statistics of Pakistan 2010-11* (Islamabad: Statistics Division, Pakistan Bureau of Statistics, 2011), p. 255.

Losses to Social Infrastructure

Housing and Settlements

The floods caused total or partial damage to more than 1.6 million housing units across the country. An estimated 9,13,307 houses were completely destroyed and another 6,94,878 partially damaged. As expected, the extent of damage incurred to *katcha* houses (generally made of mud, wood and thatch) was far higher at 19.0 per cent of the pre-disaster *katcha* housing stock (1.45 million housing units), out of which, 8,47,456 *katcha* housing units were completely destroyed. This left thousands of families without shelter and prone to hardships and diseases. Among provinces, the housing stock in Sindh was the worst affected, with almost 8,80,000 housing units completely or partially damaged, which is 55 per cent of the total affected housing stock across the country. In Punjab and KP total number of damaged houses were 3,75,773 and 2,57,294 or 23.37 and 16 per cent of total affected houses in the country respectively. Balochistan suffered a damage of 79,720 houses which made 14 of pre-floods stock (Table 9).

By contrast, only three per cent of total *pucca* housing (made of fire bricks, cement and with sufficient use of iron) stock (1,56,517 housing units) suffered damage in the country, with 65,851 being completely destroyed. Of total damaged houses, *pucca* houses made only 9.73 per cent. In FATA and GB no *pucca* house was recorded to have suffered any damage. These figures indicate the vulnerability of *katcha* houses to floods. Overall, 13 per cent houses of the total housing stock in the flood-affected districts were affected by these floods.[45] According to a rough estimate, if five persons dwell in one house, then at least eight million persons or 4.5 per cent population of Pakistan was rendered shelterless.

The direct damage to housing, reflecting the depreciated value of the affected stock, was estimated at US $ 1,080.5 million (US $ 795.3 million for completely destroyed houses and US $ 285.2 million for partially damaged houses). Indirect losses including: depreciated value of housing assets, appliances and fixtures; value of damaged water and sanitation infrastructure; cost of debris removal and demolition; and cost of providing temporary shelter to affected households,

45. WB, ADB & Government of Pakistan, Op. Cit., p. 88.

were estimated to be US $ 507.9 million. Thus, total damage to housing stock was estimated at US $ 1,588.4 million which accounts for 15.79 per cent of the total losses. As far as value of direct damage is concerned Sindh with 58.27 loss was the worst affected followed by Punjab (20.29 per cent), KP (14.20 per cent) and Balochistan (6.22 per cent) province. Thus, almost all (98.98 per cent) direct damage was reported from these provinces only. Figures of indirect damage also follow the same pattern with Sindh being worst affected followed by Punjab, KP and Balochistan. The total loss recorded as a result of damage to housing and settlements in FATA and GB was only US $ 2.2 million (Table 10).

The reconstruction and repair needs for the housing sector were calculated for the three options ranging between US $ 1.483 and 2.206 billion. Option one, costing US $ 1.483 billion is a base case, providing for a uniform subsidy for Building-As-Before (BAB) calculated on the basis of a *katcha* core unit. This option has been recommended for comparison purposes only. Option two, costing US $ 1.690.29 billion, offers a Partially Differential Subsidy (PDS) providing for restoration to flood resistant standard for those units that are located within the flood area. It has been recommended only for districts in Punjab and Sindh that are not at seismic risk. Option three, costing US $ 2.206 billion, provides for a Differential Subsidy (DS) for BAB applying multi-hazard-resistant standards for units at risk of flood and/or earthquake while building as usual in non-risk prone areas. It is the recommended option providing for optimal use of scarce public resources, while ensuring adequate hazard resistance proportionate with the relative hazard risk exposure and structural vulnerability of houses in the affected districts (Table 10).

Health Sector

The floods resulted in mild to moderate damage to the country's public health infrastructure, including basic health units and dispensaries, which suffered the most damage. However, most of the secondary healthcare facilities were unaffected. Out of a total 9,721 health facilities, 515 (5.29 per cent of the total) were partially or completely destroyed. KP with 190 (10.93 per cent) and Sindh with 151 (11.65 per cent) health facilities damaged or destroyed were worst affected among the provinces of Pakistan. FATA stands third with 8.24 per cent of its health facilities being partially or completely destroyed. In POK, total 39 or 6.30 per cent health facilities were affected by hazardous floods. Damage to health facilities in the rest of the country was calculated at 2 per cent or less (Table 11). The breakdown of the total monetary loss (direct and indirect damage) among the provinces and regions was estimated as: Punjab US $ 4.78 million, Sindh US $ 22.6 million, KP US $ 16.65 million, Balochistan US $ 2.18 million, POK US $ 2.35 million, Gilgit-Baltistan US $ 0.03 million, and FATA US $ 1.08 million. Thus, total loss at the national level was estimated at US $ 49.67 million. It also includes an indirect loss of US $ 31.30 million.[46] In the DNA, indirect losses are income losses, and include both the change of flow of goods and services and other economic flows such as increased expenses, curtailed production and diminished revenue, which arise from the direct damage to production capacity and social and economic infrastructure.

The short, medium and long-term needs for the reconstruction of this sector were estimated at US $ 48.84 million.[47] An amount of US $ 12.1 million was designated to implement the short-term strategy, while US $ 36.74 million were set for the medium and long-term reconstruction and rehabilitation of damaged health facilities (Table 11). A short-term strategy included focus on establishing essential health service packages (primary health care, emergency obstetric care, response to disease outbreak, supply of essential medical supplies, etc.). Cross-cutting issues such as care for particularly vulnerable groups (women of reproductive age, children and the elderly) were identified to be addressed as a priority. In the medium and long-term, a comprehensive health sector revitalization strategy was prepared aimed at the provision of minimum standards for healthcare, based on the key principles of equitable access to essential healthcare, timeliness, results, and accountability.

Education Sector

The unprecedented floods damaged a total of 10,407 educational institutions in the country, of which 3,741 were recorded as fully destroyed and 6,666 as partially damaged. These institutions comprise 6.2 per cent of the total institutions in the country and 12 per cent of the total institutions in the affected districts. The

46. Ibid., p. 100.
47. Ibid., p. 101.

partially damaged institutions constituted around 64 per cent of the total damaged institutions. Damage to educational institutions had affected around 32,000 teachers and 1.04 million students (0.42 million girls).[48] The two worst affected provinces (in terms of numbers of affected educational institutions) were Sindh and Punjab, where 18.5 per cent and 8.8 per cent of the pre-flood educational facilities were damaged or destroyed. In Baluchistan and KP this loss had been to the extent of 12.9 per cent and 5.6 per cent of their pre-flood educational facilities respectively.

In terms of monetary value total loss incurred to the education sector was estimated at US $ 311.34 million. Among provinces Sindh suffered a total loss of US $ 157.12 million or 50.47 per cent of the total. Punjab and KP lost US $ 92.73 and 33.64 million respectively due to damages to this sector. POK, Balochistan, FATA and GB together accounted for a total loss of US $ 27.88 million or 8.95 per cent of the total damage to this sector. Given the condition of the economy, it was very difficult for the federal and provincial governments to rebuild and repair these institutions even after a period of three years (Table 12).

Recovery needs estimated for this sector were set as high as US $ 504.8 million including US $ 63.7 million for short-term needs. The short-term requirements were aimed at ensuring the continuation of educational process in the affected districts. Long-term reconstruction needs were estimated at US $ 441.13 million (Table 12). It included reviewing of some of the policy aspects, e.g. location of schools in terms of accessibility and maximum utility and involvement of school management committees/parents teachers associations in rehabilitation and repair work.

Losses to Physical Infrastructure

Irrigation and Flood Management

The total damage to irrigation and flood protection facilities were estimated at US $ 277.65 million. A major share of the damage (US $ 136.92 million) was reported from Sindh province followed by KP (US $ 68.35 million) and Punjab

48. Ibid., p. 106.

(US $ 33.09 million). Total value of damage in rest of the country accounted for US $ 34.38 million only. Damage to the Water and Power Development Authority (WAPDA) facilities was estimated at US $ 4.89 million (Table 13). These damage estimates reflected the reconstruction requirement at depreciated value as most of the sector's affected infrastructure was more than fifty years old. Indirect losses such as damage to crops due to flooding and disruption of irrigation supplies, siltation and water-logging of agricultural land are covered and described under the agriculture sector.

The cost of the short-term (ranging 6-12 months) measures which includes restoration of canals, drains and public tube-wells, and strengthening vulnerable and damaged components of barrages and river training works was estimated at US $ 155.39 million. The medium-term programme included reconstruction of significantly damaged infrastructure and building-back-safer measures against floods. This programme was expected to be completed within a period of 2-3 years at an estimated cost of US $ 826.95 million. The total cost of recovery and reconstruction was estimated at US $ 982.36 million. Reconstruction needs of this sector in KP (US $ 600.34 million) and Sindh (US $ 210.65 million) only, amounts to 61.11 and 21.44 per cent of the total requirement. For the restoration of this sector in other provinces and areas, only US $ 171.37 million (17.45 per cent of the total) were estimated (Table 13).

Transport and Communications

The transport and communications sector consists of various categories of roads, railways, bridges, civil airports, and telecommunications infrastructure. Preliminary estimates had indicated that 10 per cent of the road network (25,090.5 km) and 16 per cent of the railways (1,225 km) were damaged by the floods. Total number of the affected motorways or national highways was 793 and most of them were reported from KP (402) and Sindh (265) only. As far as damage to other types of roads and their total lengths are concerned, these two provinces suffered the most followed by POK, Punjab, Balochistan, FATA and GB (Table 14). The disruption to the road and rail network had a two-fold impact on the mobility of the affected population. First, it made returning to the villages difficult and, after returning, access to markets and basic services also became difficult. While some of the national highways and rail network were restored in the short-term, the district and municipal roads network still continue to hamper rehabilitation and accessibility.

Total monetary loss incurred to this sector was estimated at US $ 1.328 billion which includes US $ 735.19 million as direct damage and US $ 593.18 million as indirect damage. Within this sector, the roads sustained the highest damage (US $ 1.23 billion) followed by the railways (US $ 60.09 million). Damage to telecommunication infrastructure includes loss of optical fibre transmission lines, feeder cables and, in some cases, transmission towers and equipment (US $ 35.24 million). The civil aviation sector sustained only minor damage of US $ 0.66 million (Table 15).

In view of huge losses incurred to this sector, reconstruction estimates had been set at US $ 2.356 billion with a share of the road sub-sector as US $ 2.07 billion. Total reconstruction and restoration requirements of this sector included US $ 1,834.41 million for rehabilitation and reconstruction cost, US $ 110.07 million for social safeguards, US $ 146.75 million for project management and capacity building and US $ 220.13 million for escalation cost (Table 15).

Water Supply and Sanitation

This sector had suffered a direct damage of US $ 37.58 million and indirect losses being almost double at US $ 71.91 million. Thus, total loss incurred to this sector was US $ 109.48 million. Most of the losses to this sector were reported from Sindh province only with 47.34 per cent direct and 55.46 indirect damages. Other provinces, where water and sanitation facilities had suffered damage due to severe floods were Punjab and KP with total losses of US $ 21.59 and US $ 19.80 million respectively (Table 16).

Recovery needs for this sector had been estimated as US $ 93.90 million for physical reconstruction, including priority enhancements for technical efficiency, to protect against future disasters, and to enhance sustainability of recovery investments (Table 16). Short-term priorities were estimated at US $ 39.57 million to clean up and undertake priority repairs; followed by planning and designing for better or smarter replacements or modifications of infrastructure. The cost of medium and long term actions was estimated at US $ 54.33 million. These actions were recommended based on the strong foundation of baseline service data, asset inventories and build as before recommendations.[49]

Energy Sector

In the power sector, most of the direct damage had been to the distribution networks and the hydroelectric power generation stations. As a result of the damage to distribution and transmission networks 1,06,299 customer connections were completely destroyed and another 27,421 connections were partially affected. In the petroleum sector, only 10 petrol stations and 5 CNG stations were completely destroyed while most of the infrastructure and facilities were partially affected. Total damage to the energy sector was estimated at US $ 309.40 million. This comprises a direct damage of US $ 155.09 million and indirect damage of US $ 154.30 million. Loss to power generation facilities was estimated at US $ 110.34 million or 35.66 per cent of the total loss. Total loss to oil and gas sector includes downstream gas (US $ 72.78 million), downstream oil (US $ 47.52 million) and upstream oil and gas with and amount of US $ 34.58 million. In terms of monetary loss, total damage had almost equally affected the power sector (US $ 154.52 million) and the petroleum sector with an amount of US $ 154.88 million (Table 17 & 18).

The total reconstruction needs for energy sector had been estimated at US $ 106.3 million. This amount covers direct damage to the public sector power companies and an additional amount of US $ 10 million for capacity building. Total reconstruction and rehabilitation/repair cost of the power sector was estimated at US $ 73.79 million only. An additional amount of US $ 10 million was also added to this amount to cover charges for capacity building. Total monetary requirements for the petroleum sector public companies were estimated at US $ 32.54 million. Total reconstruction needs of oil and gas sector were estimated at US $ 96.33 million excluding an additional amount of US $ 10 million for capacity building (Table 18).

49. Ibid., p. 142.

Losses to Economic and Livelihood Sectors

Agriculture, Livestock and Fisheries

Severe damages to agriculture, livestock and fisheries were reported from various parts of the country. Total 2,092.64 thousand hectare crop area was damaged. Sindh and Punjab with 1,043.5 and 746.9 thousand hectares cropped area being damaged were worst affected provinces. These floods killed 315.61 thousand large animals out of them 139.6 thousand or 44.23 per cent were lost in Balochistan alone. Around 1.21 million small animals were also lost in these floods and Balochistan accounted for 85.79 per cent of them. More than 13,000 water courses were damaged, and most of the damage was reported from Sindh and Punjab province. An amount of US $ 722.74 million was also lost due the damage to fisheries; household stocks of food, seed and feed; agriculture machinery and tools; government buildings and infrastructure facilities (Table 19).

In monetary terms, the total loss to this sector was estimated at about US $ 5.044 billion. Among the provinces, Sindh had suffered most accounting for 46 per cent of total losses followed by Punjab (36 per cent), KP (8 per cent), Balochistan (8 per cent) and the rest being reported from POK and GB. Total value of damaged crops accounted for US $ 4,473.75 million or more than 89 per cent of total losses. Livestock damage accounted for around 11 per cent of total damage. Fisheries and pond damage were more severe in Punjab where total loss to this sector was US $ 3.75 million or 83.71 per cent of the total losses to this sector. Some minor damages to fisheries and ponds were reported from Sindh and KP also but, no monetary loss to this sector was reported from POK, GB and Balochistan (Table 20).

The estimated recovery/reconstruction needs of this sector vary between US $ 257.4 million to 1.048 billion. These needs were estimated for three scenarios (low, medium and high cost) and include the costs for bringing normalcy in the agriculture sector and strengthening key government policies related to management of floods and riverine areas. Estimates were also made about the interventions for improving key policy and regulatory frameworks. The given range is from the lowest to the highest costing scenario. Crops had been worst affected, and for their recovery, an amount of US $ 754.00 million was estimated according to the high cost option.

For the low cost option, only US $ 161.00 million were estimated. For the recovery of losses to livestock, a high cost amount was estimated at US $ 194.00 million. Rest of the amount was estimated for on-farm water management, fisheries and policy-related matters (Table 21).

An analysis of the province-wise cost of restoring normalcy and rebuilding agriculture and rural livelihood for three different scenarios reveals large variations. According to low compensation scenario, an amount of only US $ 237.44 million was estimated to be sufficient for restoring normalcy and rebuilding agriculture and rural livelihood. For medium compensation scenario which was the preferred option also, an amount of US $ 649.77 million was set to meet the expenditure on restoration and rebuilding this sector. Estimated amount for high compensation scenario was US $ 1,028.64 million. According to medium compensation scenario, restoration and rebuilding work in Sindh province required US $ 266.45 million or 41 per cent of the total amount. For agriculturally developed Punjab this amount was set at US $ 159.64 million or 24.57 per cent of the total amount. Agriculture, livestock and fisheries in Balochistan were also badly affected by the devastating floods, and for the restoration and rebuilding of this sector in the province an amount of US $ 132.60 million was estimated. Rest of the amount was earmarked for the restoration and rebuilding of this sector in KP, GB, FATA and the POK (Table 22).

Private Sector and Industries

The major industrial hubs of the country remained largely unaffected by the floods, but it had seriously damaged micro, small and medium enterprises in manufacturing, trade and services sectors in the affected districts. Total 146 industrial units in KP, Punjab and Sindh were damaged. Small enterprises, businessman and shopkeepers were badly affected by these floods. According to estimates 1,19,572 units of shops and hotels were lost due to widespread floods mostly in Sindh, Punjab and KP. In KP, 236 mines were also affected by the flooding. In terms of money, total loss incurred to this sector was estimated at US $ 281.54 million. Out of the total loss, direct damage to this sector was estimated at US $ 170.15 million and indirect damage/losses at US $ 111.39 million. The province of

Sindh was the worst affected as it lost US $ 138.29 million or more than 49 per cent of the total loss to this sector. Rest of the damage was reported from Punjab, KP and Balochistan. Recovery/reconstruction needs of private sector and industries were estimated at US $ 102 to 129 million following a holistic and integrated approach (Table 23).

Financial Sector

An assessment of the total damage and losses to the financial sector was primarily made on the basis of the impact of the floods on the banking, micro-finance, and the Non-Bank Financial Institutions (NBFI) sector with particular focus on the insurance industry. The total physical damage to this sector had been estimated at US $ 1.29 million out of which a monetary loss amounting to around US $ 0.89 million had been to the commercial banking sector and US $ 0.40 million to micro-finance institutions (MFIs). The total loan losses due to floods were estimated at about US $ 672.21 million. The loan losses of the banking sector (US $ 616.90 million) constituted 91 per cent of the total losses while the remainder was reported from the MFIs and the insurance and leasing sectors. The largest share of loan losses of 55 per cent was of the agriculture sector, while losses of small and medium enterprise (SMEs) and housing were 20 and 4 per cent respectively. Amongst the provinces the largest share of losses to this sector had been of Punjab (63 per cent) followed by Sindh (19 per cent) and KP (13 per cent). While banks' non-performing loans (NPLs) in the affected areas were more than double, still they were not that significant as a proportion of their overall portfolio of outstanding loans. However, the Zarai Taraqiati Bank Limited, a specialised agriculture bank, alone represented about 38 per cent of the total NPLs in the affected districts and had faced capital constraints. Total recovery/reconstruction needs of this sector were estimated at US $ 463.04 million. Financially, those banks which were the worst affected by the floods required US $ 423.6 million for recovery. Rest of the amount of US $ 39.44 million was estimated for the micro-finance sector.[50]

50. Ibid., p. 32.

Social Protection and Livelihoods

More than 19 million persons were affected in 78 districts of Pakistan. Punjab and Sindh with 38.42 and 35.38 per cent of the total affected population, were severely affected provinces of the country. It indicates that most of the affected population was concentrated in eastern and southern parts of Pakistan. More than 15 per cent of the affected population was reported from KP in northern part of the country. Thus, around 89 per cent population was affected in these three provinces only. Other provinces constituted only 11 per cent of the affected population. Total affected population was living in 2.9 million households out of which 1.9 million (66 per cent) were severely affected. Again out of total affected households more than 2.2 million were reported from Sindh and Punjab only. Therefore, more attention was needed in southern parts of the country for taking care of social protection and livelihoods. As far as severity of the affected households is concerned, almost 77 per cent households were severely affected in Sindh, KP and Balochistan. At the national level 64.15 per cent households were severely affected according to specification one. According to specification two, 66.32 per cent households were severely affected (Table 25).

As far as estimates for cash grants to severely affected households is concerned, according to specification one, an amount of US $ 654 million was estimated for addressing the short-term needs of severely affected households for a period of six months. According to specification two, this amount was estimated as US $ 683 million. For severely affected Sindh, an amount of US $ 306.9 million (44.93 per cent of the total) was estimated as cash grants. For severely affected households in Punjab and KP this amount was set at US $ 215.6 million and US $ 100.3 million respectively. For other provinces and regions, an amount of only US $ 60.4 million was distributed as cash grants (Table 25).

Losses to Cross-cutting Sectors

According to the damage and need analysis report, crosscutting sectors includes governance institutions, environment and disaster risk management (DRM). A detailed study of the losses to the environment has already been carried out separately to emphasize the importance of this sector. In any country of the world, failure of the governance institutions and disaster risk management system at the time of the tragedy may multiply the severity and losses. Therefore, a detailed study of the losses to these sectors is essential for a comprehensive understanding of the impact of floods in Pakistan also.

Governance

The devastating floods of 2010 had damaged hundreds of governance institutions with a total loss of US $ 70.31 million. It included US $ 36.96 million lost due to direct damage and US $ 33.35 million due to indirect impact of the floods. An analysis of the province-wise distribution of direct damage reveals that Sindh (US $ 21.92 million) and KP (US $ 11.51 million) had been worst-affected. Rest of the losses were reported from other parts of country. Local government infrastructure and post offices were hit the hardest. KP, Sindh and Punjab police operations were affected by the floodwater. Across the country, important documents, papers including land records had suffered damages. Normal functioning of the government was severely hampered by these floods. Broadly, capacity to govern, provide assistance and start reconstruction activities had been severely hampered. Internally displaced persons (IDPs) entitlements were under risk and the public security was worrisome especially in Sindh, KP and Punjab. Most of the indirect losses were also reported from these provinces only (Table 26).

Recovery and reconstruction needs for governance infrastructure were estimated at US $ 57.65 million. This cost included rebuilding vital infrastructure and improving the procurement, public financial management and institutional systems within the public sector to support the provincial and local governments during reconstruction. Of the total amount, nearly US $ 13.30 million had been estimated for restoring and augmenting state capacities to deal with the post-disaster situation. For recovery from the damage US $ 34.19 million and US $ 17.96 million were required in Sindh and KP respectively. For other provinces and regions, an amount of US $ 5.51 million was needed for recovery and normal functioning of governance institutions (Table 26).

Disaster Risk Management

As mentioned earlier no estimates of direct and indirect losses have been made about disaster risk management. But, it is possible to make some estimates about the losses incurred in sectors like irrigation, agriculture and livestock, etc. According to available data at least US $ 27 million were estimated for disaster risk management.[51]

51. Ibid., p. 59.

5. Floods Impact Assessment

The impact of floods can be studied in two ways. First is immediate and direct losses and another category consists of after-effects which continue to hamper recovery and normalcy for a very long period of time. A detailed analysis of the immediate and direct losses of the floods has been carried out earlier. Here, an attempt is made to assess and analyse the after-effects or impact ensuing from the direct losses to different sectors of the economy, environmental and ecosystem services.

Environment and Ecosystem Services

Ecosystem services are defined in terms of the benefits that people derive from the natural environment. These range from food, fibre and timber production to the natural regulation of floods, from soaking up carbon dioxide to providing a place for living and recreation. Different types of ecosystem services include provisioning services: tangible physical and energetic goods obtained from ecosystem, e.g. food and fibre; regulatory services: benefits obtained from ecosystem processes that regulate aspects of the environment, e.g. air quality, climate and water regulation; cultural services: non-material benefits people obtain from ecosystem, e.g. recreation, aesthetic experiences, health and wellb-eing; supporting services: services comprising internal processes within ecosystems essential for the production of all other ecosystem services, e.g. soil formation, primary production, nutrient cycling.[52] No life can be imagined in the absence of these services; therefore, for an early recovery and management of the environment it is pertinent that a comprehensive assessment of the losses incurred to this sector be made after the occurance of any disaster.

52. Millennium Ecosystem Assessment, *Ecosystems and Human Wellbeing: A Framework for Assessment* (Washington, DC: Island Press, 2003), pp. 3-5.

As far as the impact of floods is concerned it is very difficult to separate their environmental consequences from the economic consequences. For example loss of crops, animals, houses, forests, etc., have both environmental as well as economic consequences. All lost or damaged infrastructure facilites have to be developed again using resources from the environment. Therefore, it may also be argued that all damages and losses are actually of the environment itself. What follows is a detailed analysis of the impact of the 2010 floods on the environment and the economy of Pakistan. After more than two years, many of the environmental and economic consequences of the floods are more evident. In normal conditions also, annual loss to environment in Pakistan is very high. In 2006, according to a study of the World Bank, the mean estimated annual cost of environmental and natural resource damage was about US $ 6.05 billion per year or 6 per cent of the GDP. This figure, when calculated at 2010 conversion value of the Pakistani Rupee amounts to US $ 8.52 billion per year (Table 27). The widespread floods of 2010 had affected every region and sector of the economy; therefore, it may have certainly increased environmental costs much beyond this figure and disturbed it's functioning. No comprehensive study has yet been conducted to exactly measure the total monetary loss to the environment and its services.

Pakistan also suffers a loss of 8.84 per cent of its GDP each year from environment-related diseases. Almost half of this cost is caused by mortality (4.13 per cent of GDP) while the rest stems from the malnutrition caused by environment-related diseases (4.71 per cent of GDP). Approximately 90 per cent of typhoid and diarrheal illness in Pakistan is attributable to inadequate drinking water, sanitation and hygiene.[53] Widespread diseases and deaths in Pakistan during floods may have increased this figure much beyond the normal losses. Many areas of Pakistan remained plunged for many weeks and thousands of people including women and children remained without shelter and medicines. Many of them died due to diseases and lack of proper care.

Floods have both nurturing as well as destructive potentials for affecting the environment and economy. The destructive impact of floods affects environment in both long as well as short terms. Therefore, environmental destruction of the 2010

53. Ministry of Finance, Government of Pakistan, *Economic survey of Pakistan 2011-2012* (Islamabad: Economic Adviser's Wing, Finance Division, 2012), p. 254.

floods will continue to affect the life of people and health of the environment for many more years. Contaminated water, loss of flora and fauna and their habitats, erosion and pollution of soil, diseases and loss of human life are some of the results of destructive environmental impact of these floods. And, it is very difficult to exactly measure destructive environmental impact in the absence of reliable data and research. As far as nurturing impact is concerned, flood water offers diverse ecosystem services that are vital for the natural environment. In the case of most Pakistani rivers, short periods of inundation caused by average seasonal floods deliver valuable silt to the farmlands, thus enriching them both physically and chemically. They recharge the soil, ponds, lakes and groundwater aquifers. It is mainly because of these reasons that wheat crop recorded a bumper crop of 24.2 million tons in 2011 compared with the previous 23.8 million tons in 2010. Yield of cotton also increased from 707 kg/ha to 725 kg/ha during this period. Sugarcane, one of the major cash crops of Pakistan also achieved highest yield of 55,981 kg/ha which was 6.9 per cent higher than that of the previous year. During 2010-11, the production of *bajra*, tobacco, rapeseed and mustard, maize and barley also increased by 18.1 per cent, 16 per cent, 11.3 per cent, 2.4 per cent and 2.8 per cent, respectively.[54]

Following floods, price related inflation stimulated production of many minor crops, resulting in that sub-sector expanding at a rate of 4.8 per cent. Despite the great flood-related loss of livestock, the sector still expanded at 3.7 per cent in comparison to 4.2 per cent in the previous year.[55] Floods also transport fish population over large distances. The Himalayan and other rivers deposit thousands of tons of fertile soils in central and southern parts of the country. Big floods are also essential for keeping the river channel free of silt, in the absence of which the carrying capacity of the rivers would get reduced and the basin would become flood-prone. Floods recharge water storage areas, thus helping sustain riparian plants and animals in areas away from the river. The role of annual floodwaters in sustaining the constantly changing complex physical and biological processes on the floodplains has been utilised in the traditional agricultural practices. The intensity and extent of flooding vary from year to year. Thus, in the years with

54. Ministry of Finance, Government of Pakistan, *Economic Survey of Pakistan 2010-2011*, Op. Cit., pp. 15-33.
55. Ibid., p. 6-7.

catastrophic flooding and long periods of inundations, more economic damages are inflicted. Such major floods in the plains, for instance, with a return period of more than 100 years, together with flash floods in upland watersheds have been responsible for more deaths and devastations.[56]

As far as the economic impact of the floods is concerned, even before the catastrophic floods, Pakistan's economy was under considerable stress. The government's debt had reached over US $ 55 billion. The tax base in the country is very narrow, and a third of the population is living below the poverty line.[57] Apart from this, since 2001, the war on terrorism had inflicted the country with a loss of around US $ 67.93 billion. In 2010-2011 alone, terrorism had caused some US $17.82 billion loss to the country. An unexpected loss of US $ 10 billion due to the floods had further strained fiscal resources. Rising inflation, increased defense spending, reduced subsidies and acute power shortages had negatively impacted rural and urban wages, private demand, manufacturing activity and public spending on economic development (already an extremely low percentage of the budget). Compounding government's problems had contributed to a significant drop in private investment critically needed for recovery and employment creation. For the economy as a whole, the floods were responsible for a reduction in the GDP growth by about 2 percentage points.[58] A detailed sector-wise analysis of the impact of the 2010 floods follows.

Economy and Development

Agriculture Sector and Food Security

Due to widespread destruction, the agricultural sector recorded a modest growth of 1.2 per cent in 2010-11 against the target of 3.8 per cent. All standing crops and the cultivation of *rabi* crops were affected by the floods. Total area

56. U.C. Sharma, "Land-Use Options for the Floodplains of the North-Eastern Region of India," in Fiona J. Dyer, Martin C. Thoms and Jon M. Olley (eds.), *The Structure, Function and Management Implications of Fluvial Sedimentary Systems,* Publication No. 276 (Oxfordshire: International Association of Hydrological Sciences, 2002), pp. 239-44, and J. Bandyopadhyay, *Water, Ecosystems and Society: A Confluence of Disciplines* (New Delhi: Sage Publications India Pvt. Ltd., 2009), pp. 55-56.
57. A. Rodriguez, "Pakistan's Economy Barely Afloat," *The Los Angeles Times*, 19 September 2010.
58. Ministry of Finance, Government of Pakistan, *Economic Survey of Pakistan 2010-2011,* Op. Cit., p. 1 and pp. 218-20.

under food-grains registered a negative growth from 13,758 thousand hectares in 2009-10 to 13,094 thousand hectares in 2010-11.The destruction of rice and cotton crops, led to a negative growth of 4.0 per cent in major crops. Among major crops, area under rice declined sharply from 2,883 thousand hectares in 2009-10 to 2,365 thousand hectares in 2010-11. It had a direct impact on the total production of rice in Pakistan which declined to 4.823 million tons, the lowest level since 2001-02 (Table 28). Forestry, which has great environmental and economic value, also continued its historical negative growth and declined by 0.4 per cent. Despite price rise of many crops and the subsequent increase in rural incomes, agriculture's flood-related difficulties had an effect on the flow of credit to that sector. Accordingl to available data, credit flow to agriculture sector had increased marginally by 1.4 per cent from July 2010 through March 2011.[59]

Due to the loss of food-grains and delay in sowing wheat, the food security of millions of Pakistani was at risk. In spite of improvement in water and moisture availability due to widespread floods and consequential increase in wheat sown area in non-irrigated as well as canal fed areas (that accounted for approximately 87 per cent of the total area under wheat cultivation), total area under wheat cultivation had declined to 8,901 thousand hectares from 9,132 thousand hectares in 2009-10. But, the improvement in the yield of wheat from 2,553 kg/ha in 2009-10 to 2,760 kg/ha in 2010-11 more than compensated the loss of area and total production increased to 25,214 tons in 2010-11 (Table 28). The Food Agriculture Organization (FAO) had even warned the Pakistan government of severe consequences of food shortage in September 2010 as around 77 million people were without sufficient food during the floods.[60] Even after the recession of the floods in December 2010, food prices remained high and Pakistan had to go through a difficult transition to recovery.

Poor farmers whose income's major share was derived from livestock and cattle rearing were also severely devastated by the floods. For these farmers, livestock

59. Ibid., p. iii and pp. 6-25.
60. M. Kugelman, "Pakistan's Food Insecurity: Roots, Ramifications, and Responses," in M. Kugelman and R. M. Hathaway (eds.), *Hunger Pains: Pakistan's Food Insecurity* (Washington, D.C.: Woodrow Wilson International Center for Scholars, 2010), p. 8; Pakistan Institute for Peace Studies, *Pakistan Security Report 2010* (Islamabad: January 2011), p. 42, and Ministry of Finance, Government of Pakistan, *Economic Survey of Pakistan 2011-2012,* Op. Cit., p. 22.

and cattle are not only the source of income but food and milk also. They had lost a big share of their livestock and cattle. Farmers of Sindh and KP had particularly suffered major losses. As a consequence, per capita household losses of poultry at the national level were reported up to 72 per cent while in Sindh this figure was as high as 83 per cent. After floods, average losses of buffaloes, sheep/goats and cows were 40 per cent, 39 per cent and 38 per cent respectively (Table 29). As per the records of the Ministry of National Food Security and Research, Pakistan, this decline in the average number of livestock per household was temporary as there was no decline in the total number of livestock at national level in 2010-11.[61]

Manufacturing Sector

In Pakistan manufacturing includes, large-scale manufacturing, small-scale manufacturing and slaughtering.[62] The growth of manufacturing sector was adversely affected by weak performance of textiles and chronic energy shortages. Widespread destruction of cotton crop adversely affected the performance of textile sector. Further, the non-recovery of informal credit extended to cotton farmers and the increase in production costs due to use of imported cotton had reduced the competitiveness of Pakistani textile products in international markets. Textile industry contributes about 60 per cent to the total export earnings of the country and accounts for 46 per cent of the total manufacturing and provides employment to 38 per cent of the labour involved in manufacturing.

As an indirect effect, reduced purchasing power of flood victims who made almost 20 per cent of the population of Pakistan may have affected the performance of this sector. Simultaneously, higher agricultural prices stemming from flood shortages resulted in a significant transfer of resources to rural areas, much of which went towards the purchase of consumer durables.[63] These reasons may be largely attributed to decline in the growth rate of manufacturing sector to 3.06

61. Ministry of Finance, Government of Pakistan, *Economic Survey of Pakistan 2011-2012,* Op. Cit., p. 36.
62. Pakistan Bureau of Statistics, Government of Pakistan, *National Accounts of Pakistan Rebasing From 1980-81 to 1999-2000* (Islamabad: Ministry of Economic Affairs & Statistics, Statistics Division, 2003), p.2. Available at http://www.pbs.gov.pk/sites/default/files/national_accounts/publications/rebase_national_accounts/writeup/chapter1.pdf (Accesses on 27 November 2011).
63. Ministry of Finance, Government of Pakistan, *Economic Survey of Pakistan 2010-2011,* Op. Cit., p. i and pp. 34-36.

per cent in 2010-11 from 5.46 per cent in the previous year. Though, small and medium scale manufacturing maintained its growth rate of 7.5 per cent in 2010-11 also. As for the future, the government's ongoing budgetary difficulties are likely to result in lower investment in rural employment generation; lower prices paid to farmers and potentially lower rural incomes. This together with reoccurrence of floods points to the vulnerability of the agriculture and manufacturing nexus. In Sindh and Punjab, cotton ginning, sugar, rice processing and flour mills were the main sectors damaged by the floods. In KP, affected industries were that of marble, furniture, silk, horticulture, mining and tourism.[64]

Service Sector

The service sector in Pakistan includes transport, storage and communication; wholesale & retail trade; finance and insurance; ownership of dwellings; public administration & defence; and social, community and private services.[65] This sector constitutes 53.3 per cent of the economy of the country. Therefore, even a slight change in the growth of this sector is likely to have greater impact on the economy of Pakistan. This sector's growth at 4.1 per cent during 2010-11 as opposed to the original target of 4.7 per cent and actual outcome of 2.9 per cent was directly or indirectly affected by widespread floods.[66]

Finance and insurance sector had recorded a negative growth of 6.3 per cent in 2010-11 as against the reduction of 11.3 per cent in previous year. The transport, storage and communication sub-sector depicted a sharp deceleration in growth continuing for the last three years and grew by 1.3 per cent only. Among these sub-sectors communication had declined by 12.1 per cent and pipeline transport by 15.9 per cent. Against the set target of 5.1 per cent in 2010-11, the wholesale and retail trade sector grew at 3.9 per cent as compared to 4.6 per cent in 2009-10. Public administration and defence recorded a growth of 13.2 per cent in 2010-11 as compared to 2.5 per cent in 2009-10, mainly due to a positive change in

64. Ibid., p. iii and p. 8; Planning Commission, Government of Pakistan, *National Flood Reconstruction Plan 2010* (Islamabad: Government of Pakistan, 2011), p. 46, and Ministry of Finance, Government of Pakistan, *Economic Survey of Pakistan 2011-2012,* Op. Cit., p. 5.
65. Pakistan Bureau of Statistics, Government of Pakistan, *National Accounts of Pakistan,* Op. Cit., p.2
66. Ministry of Finance, Government of Pakistan, *Economic Survey of Pakistan 2010-2011,* Op. Cit., p. i and pp. 6-8.

the wage component of public sector employees, and an increase in defence and security related expenditures. Growth in the ownership of dwellings had remained constant at 3.5 per cent in 2010-11 also, due to the negative impact of some other factors including floods. Social services sector grew by 7.1 per cent which is higher than the target of 5.0 per cent but lower than 2009-10 actual growth of 7.8 per cent. These figures also indicate direct or indirect impact of the floods on the service sector of Pakistan.[67]

Due to the floods, non-performing loans (NPL) also increased with the NPL to loan ratio reaching 14 per cent by September 2010. The most vulnerable sectors were small and medium enterprises (SME) where the NPL to loan ratio had reached 25 per cent, in the mortgage loans and agriculture sector it had reached up to 20 per cent. Clearly, the floods had badly affected the financial system. According to available data, the amount of NPL had increased by Rs 58 billion (US $ 0.68 billion) to reach Rs 517.9 billion (US $ 6.09 billion) by the end of December 2010, against an increase of Rs 34.1 billion (US $ 0.40 billion) in the same period in 2009.[68]

Inflation and Price Rise

Disruption caused by floods had affected the whole system of demand and supply in Pakistan which had a direct impact on the availability and prices of all products and services. Therefore, inflation as measured by the changes in consumer price index (CPI) also reflected the impact of the floods. According to data, CPI had increased by 14.1 per cent in July-April 2010-11 against 11.5 per cent in the comparative period in the previous year. Table 30 shows inflation trends from December 2009 to December 2010. An analysis of these figures reveals that most inflation figures had increased between the month of July and September 2010. The CPI for general and food item had increased significantly between the month of July and September 2010. Contrarily, inflation figures for non-food items had declined suggesting their relatively lower demand. Core inflation also declined between the month of July and September 2010. WPI and SPI had increased significantly during the time of the floods in 2010, suggesting a clear impact on the economy.

67. Ibid., pp. 1-14.
68. Ibid., p. 71.

During the period of the floods, demand of food products remained the major driver of inflation including increase in the prices of imported fuel and food stuff. Food inflation was recorded at 21.2 per cent in September 2010 as against 12.8 per cent in July same year. The CPI Inflation for non-food component was recorded at 10.4 per cent for the period of July-April 2010-11 against 11 per cent in the comparable period of previous year. The non-food non-energy measure or core inflation (overall inflation adjusted for food and energy) was estimated at 9.5 per cent during July-April 2010-11 which was 11.2 per cent in the comparable period of previous year. The wholesale price index (WPI) during July-April 2010-11 increased by 23.3 per cent, as against 11.3 per cent in the same period in 2009-10. That inflation was mainly driven by upsurge in textile and energy prices. Inflation in textile sector was mainly due to the damage to cotton crops by the floods and rise in external demand for cotton related exports and massive surge in international prices. The impact of floods was also visible in manufacturing sub-groups. Among other groups of WPI suggests that in the food category, the supply shocks had adverse impact on food inflation and was more visible in prices of pulses, rice, meat, milk, sugar and vegetables, clearly associated with flood-related disruptions.[69] Due to government borrowing, inflationary pressures were quite severe even in the beginning of fiscal year 2010-11 which had worsened due to the devastating floods in the later part of the year. The widespread losses due to the floods had contributed to inflation which had reached 15.7 per cent in September 2010 from 12.3 per cent in July 2010.

Table 31 shows increase in domestic commodity prices as a result of widespread devastation caused by the floods. Prices of items like gram pulse, eggs, sugar, *gur*, potatoes, onions and garlic increased more than 20 per cent between July and September 2010. Prices of tomatoes more than doubled during floods. Many other essential commodities also registered higher increase in their prices. The direct victims of this price rise were the poor; flood affected and dislocated persons who had already lost everything to the floods.

The World Food Program (WFP) data from early 2010 also showed that the prices of essential food items in Pakistan were nearly 40 per cent higher than the

69. Ibid., pp. 93-101.

five-year cumulative averages (Table 32). In addition, a simultaneous increase in the prices of international commodities had further added to inflationary pressures. During September 2010 currency in circulation increased to Rs 1,388.8 billion as compared to Rs 1,316.5 billion in July same year. This increase in the supply of money in the absence of higher level of production may also have caused inflation and price rise.[70]

Fiscal Developments

The fiscal accounts in the country were badly affected by the floods which had forced the government to finance relief efforts, slowed overall growth and caused a significant drop in revenues. Due to the floods and poor economic condition, fiscal deficit had increased to 4.3 per cent of GDP during the months of July-March 2011 as compared to 4.2 per cent in the comparable period of 2009-10. In June 2010, total amount of direct taxes (PKR 103.7 billion) was more than the total amount collected during the months of July, August and September. As far as indirect taxes are concerned, their total amount collected during the months of floods (July, August, and September) also remained below than that collected in the month of June. One exception to this was the amount of sales tax collected during the month of August (PKR 54.2 billion), which was fairly high than that collected during the month of June 2010 (PKR 52.1 billion). Total taxes collected during the months of floods also could not reach the amount collected during the month of June. Amount of total taxes collected during the month of September (highest during the flooding period) was 116.4 billion rupees while same amount for the month of June was PKR 191.8 billion. Therefore, total tax collection in the country had declined by 39.36 per cent (Table 33).

Because of low collection of total taxes, the target for 2010-11 had to be adjusted upward from 4.0 per cent of GDP to 5.3 per cent of GDP. Financial conditions had become critical as the tax-to-GDP ratio had reached below 10 per cent being one of the lowest in the world. In March 2011, to counter these trends, the Government

70. State Bank of Pakistan, *Statistical Bulletin,* December 2010 (Islamabad: Economic Analysis Department, 2011), p. 6, and R. Looney, "Economic Impacts of the Floods in Pakistan," *Contemporary South Asia*, Vol. 20, No. 2, June 2012, pp. 225-41. Available at http://dx.doi.org/10.1080/09584935.2012.670203 (Accessed on 27 July 2013).

of Pakistan introduced three new tax measures. These included the imposition of a one-time flood-surcharge on income tax, an additional excise duty of 1 per cent on some selected luxury items and removal of exemptions on many goods subject to sales tax. The devastation caused by the floods obscured some of the optimism regarding economic resurgence and reforms. Acute energy shortages due to floods had also eclipsed prospects of growth in large-scale manufacturing, the main source of tax revenues. Consequently, the target of tax collection had to be revised downward to 4.74 per cent.[71]

Monetary Developments

Growing deficits had forced the government to borrow with financing requirements increasing from Rs 397.6 billion in 2009-10 to Rs 614.2 billion in 2010-11. The mounting fiscal deficits were largely monetized by the State Bank of Pakistan. However, rising prices stemming from flood-related food shortages had created difficulties for the Bank to finance the government's growing deficits and at the same time combat inflationary forces. Therefore, SBP had to pursue a tight monetary policy at a time when normally easy credit to revive expenditures would have been the normal policy response. Even before the floods the Bank had maintained a tight monetary policy for some time. Post-flood inflationary pressures, however forced the Bank to increase the policy rate (the SBP monetary policy rate to control inflation) to 14 per cent on 30 November 2010. The net effect of these developments was a significant drop in Pakistan's investment-to-GDP ratio from 22.5 per cent in 2006-07 to 13.4 per cent in 2010-11.[72]

Worker's remittances were also recorded at an all-time high during floods. According to data provided by the SBP, in the month of July 2010, total amount of remittances was US $ 791.18 million only, which rose to US $ 933.06 million in August. Thus, there was recorded a sharp increase of 17.93 per cent within a period of one month only. In September, amount of total remittances again came down to US $ 922.06 million. This indicates that large-scale destruction of properties and

71. Looney, "Economic Impacts of the Floods in Pakistan," Op. Cit., pp. 233-34, and Ministry of Finance, Government of Pakistan, *Economic Survey of Pakistan 2010-2011*, Op. Cit., p. vi and pp. 47- 56.
72. Ministry of Finance, Government of Pakistan, *Economic Survey of Pakistan 2010-2011*, Op. Cit., p. 62

loss of lives back home had pressurised workers to send more money for their family members.[73]

Foreign Direct Investment

Except the floods, the decline in foreign direct investment (FDI) in Pakistan has been attributed to many other factors including the deterioration in law and order, the energy crises, concerns over possible political instability and weak economic performance. Total FDI in Pakistan declined by 28.7 per cent during July-April 2010-11 as a result of fall in equity capital and re-invested earnings.[74] In July 2010, when flooding took place, total amount of FDI was US $ 109.8 million which declined to US $ 77.1 million in August. That decline may be attributed to widespread flooding and associated problems of the country. During the month of September, this amount again temporarily rose to US $ 208 million and fell down to an amount of US $ 72.9 million in the month of October. In addition, the post- flood environment with the massive destruction of infrastructure would have discouraged new investment.[75]

Health, Poverty and Deprivation

Pakistan is characterised by low levels of human development. Before the floods in 2009, according to the United Nations Human Development Index (HDI), Pakistan ranked 141 out of 182 countries. But, in 2010 when the floods occurred, its HDI rank slipped to 125 out of 169 countries, therefore, recording a fall of 3 places in the index in comparison to its level in 2009. Again in 2011, Pakistan improved its rank by two steps and ranked 145 out of 187 countries. That decline in the human development performance of the country in 2010 may partly be attributed to the devastating floods. Poverty level in Pakistan is also very high, as

---

73. State Bank of Pakistan, *Statistical Bulletin, December 2010*, Op. Cit., p. 7, and State Bank of Pakistan, *The State of Pakistan's Economy: First Quarterly Report 2010-2011* (Islamabad: Central Board of State Bank of Pakistan, 2011), p. 71.
74. Ministry of Finance, Government of Pakistan, *Economic Survey of Pakistan 2010-2011*, Op. Cit., p. xv.
75. Abdul Rehman, Muhammad Ilyas, Hassan M. Alam and Muhammad Akram, "The Impact of Infrastructure on Foreign Direct Investment: The Case of Pakistan," *International Journal of Business Management*, Vol. 6, No. 5, May 2011, pp. 268-76, and State Bank of Pakistan, *Statistical Bulletin, December 2010*, p. 7.

it is estimated that 36 per cent of the population lives on less than one US dollar a day and almost 25 per cent of the population is malnourished including up to 38 per cent of children.

The poor population suffered most due to floods, according to the United Nations Development Programme's preliminary estimates; the floods had pushed almost 4 per cent of Pakistan's population below the calorie-based poverty line, mostly in rural areas. As a result, the millennium development goal (MDG) of halving the proportion of people living under US $ 1 per day and the proportion of people suffering from hunger had become less likely to be achieved.[76] The 2010 floods had affected more than 2.8 million children under five years of age; 1.4 million of them were severely affected. Due to the spread of the incidence of diarrhea, acute respiratory infections and malaria, under five mortality rate of 89, was expected to have increased to 110-120 deaths per 1,000 live births.[77]

Unfortunately the people most severely affected by the floods were predominantly small farmers and unskilled labourers. They are among the most vulnerable in Pakistan and almost all live below or just around the national poverty line. It is estimated that 6.6 million of Pakistan's labour force was out of work for 2 to 3 months, and capital stock worth US $ 2.6 billion (1.2 per cent of GDP) was lost. More than 60 per cent of the affected population had lost access to primary livelihood and 5.3 million jobs were affected. According to the World Bank, about 2 per cent of households control more than 45 per cent of the total land area. Big farmers have also monopolized subsidies in water and agriculture which contributes heavily to rural poverty.[78]

76. M. Kugelman, Op. Cit., p. 8, and AusAid, *Australia's Strategic Approach to Aid in Pakistan, December 2010* (Barton: Government of Australia, 2010), pp. 4-5. Available at http://www.ausaid.gov.au/Publications/Documents/strat-approach-pakistan-2010.pdf, (Accessed on 13 August 2013).

77. Ministry of Finance, Government of Pakistan, *Economic Survey of Pakistan 2010-2011*, Op. Cit., p. 142, and The World We Want, *Pakistan: An Analysis of the Impact of the Floods on MDGs in Pakistan* (February 2011), pp. 43-44. Available at http://www.worldwewant2015.org/node/311136 (Accessed on 9 December 2013).

78. National Bank of Pakistan (2010), "Pakistan in the Aftermath of the Floods," *Economic Bulletin, September-October, 2010*, p. 8; State Bank of Pakistan, *Annual Report 2010-2011: The State of Pakistan's Economy* (Islamabad: Economic Policy Review Department of State Bank of Pakistan, 2011), p. 1; Ministry of Finance, Government of Pakistan, *Economic Survey of Pakistan 2010-2011*, Op. Cit., p. 221, and IRIN, "Floods Uncover Evidence of Feudalism's Impact on Poor," 17 February 2011. Available at http://www.irinnews.org/report/91952/pakistan-floods-uncover-evidence-of-feudalism-s-impact-on-poor (Accessed on 11 August 2013).

Displacement and Refugees

Prior to the floods, Pakistan already had about four million internally displaced people and refugees. About 15,50,000 more persons were displaced outside the flooded areas.[79] Several months after the floods, the situation had changed considerably from area to area. In KP and Punjab, around 95 per cent of those displaced were able to return to their homes. Even after many months of devastating floods, in Sindh province, nearly 85 per cent of the affected population had to live in refugee camps.[80] Though, the numbers of refugee camps had come down, but many of those flooded out did not return to their devastated homes, instead they had migrated to some of the country's major cities such as Karachi and Lahore. The result was increased pressure on existing infrastructure in urban areas. Lack of jobs and very poor living conditions for these migrants created many problems with crime and violence on the rise, particularly in Karachi.

79. R. A. Dixon and Teresita Schaffer, "Pakistan Floods: Internally Displaced People and the Human Impact," *South Asia Monitor* (Washington, DC: Centre for Strategic and International Studies, 2010), p. 1.
80. C. Parenti, "Pakistan One Year after the Floods," *The Nation*, 28 June 2011.

6. Conclusion

The 2010 monsoon floods were massive and unprecedented, killing 1,985 persons, affecting over 20 per cent of the land area and more than 20 million people, and causing a loss of around US $ 10.06 billion by the damages of infrastructure, housing, agriculture and livestock, and other assets. Among provinces, Sindh, Punjab and KP were severely affected contributing 80.86 per cent of the total economic losses. Most of the loss of human lives was also reported from these provinces. Between 60 and 88 per cent of the farming households, mostly located in Punjab and Sindh had reported more than 50 per cent losses to agriculture. The floods had severe impact on people's lives and livelihoods and most did not know when they would be able to resume their normal life. Many reconstruction estimates were presented to rehabilitate and normalise people's lives. According to the 'base case' that amount was estimated at US $ 6.80 billion while one 'recommended option' had set that estimate at US $ 8.91 billion. Administrative machinery at all levels had crippled to cope with such a crisis and most flooded areas remained completely disconnected from rest of the world. The international community had pledged some aid and other assistance but that was also not sufficient given the enormous economic and environmental losses. Relief efforts were lead by the Government of Pakistan and the United Nations. The NDMA along with some international NGOs also helped in relief and response stages of the disaster. Due to their efforts, some 1.5 million people were rescued by the 20,000 army/military troops deployed by November 2010. Despite many problems and the slow onset in the response many reliefs, search and rescue operations were successful. Timely distribution of food and medical assistance were generally successful in saving many lives and arresting the breakout of deadly diseases.

In the context of prevailing economic, political, social and environmental problems of the country, the flood losses of more than US $ 10 billion (5.8 per cent of the GDP for the year 2009-10) become very significant. The floods occurred when the country was still struggling to recover from the widespread damages and loss of thousands of lives caused by the earthquake of 2005. The performance of the economy had considerably lost growth momentum after that crisis. Therefore, even before the occurrence of the floods, the growth rate of the economy was very slow. Between 2007-08 and 2010-11, the average GDP growth rate was just 2.9 per cent as against 5.56 per cent in the preceding seven years. Many internal and external causes like massive terms of trade shock of 2008, global financial crisis, intensification of war on terror, security hazards and high profile killings were identified as being responsible for the deceleration of growth momentum. But, the floods of 2010 were found to be largely responsible for the significant slump in the economic performance of the country. In 2009-10, the GDP growth rate was 3.8 per cent which came down to 2.4 per cent in 2010-11 due to the floods. The after-effects of these floods were so deep and widespread that the economic environment in Pakistan remained inhospitable for growth and investment during 2010-11, and the government had to think of evolving a comprehensive growth strategy to increase productivity, efficiency, and competitiveness of the economy, and to ensure high growth rates that are both sustainable as well as more equitable.

An analysis of the sector-wise losses of the floods reveals that agriculture, labour intensive industries and housing were badly affected. As a result of this, millions of people lost their livelihood and shelters in 78 districts of the country. Around 16,08,184 housing units consisting 13 per cent of the pre-existing stock and worth of US $ 1,588.4 million were damaged. Sindh and Balochistan were particularly affected by the floods where the recorded damages were as high as 24 per cent and 14 per cent of the pre-existing stock of the houses respectively. Rural population was more severely affected because the agriculture, livestock and fisheries sector which is the main source of livelihood for millions of Pakistani, had lost US $ 5,045 billion constituting more than 50 per cent of the total losses. The severity of the losses to the agriculture sector may be gauged from the fact that more than 77 million people were without sufficient food during the floods. The poor and low wage workers were doubly affected, as they had lost employment on one hand and faced sharp price rise in household commodities on the other.

Compounding impact of losses in other sectors (totaling US $ 2,177 million) had almost broken the backbone of the economy and the rate of unemployment had increased from 5.6 per cent in 2009-10 to 6.0 per cent in 2010-11. Losses to the transport and communication sector worth US $ 1,328 million had isolated millions of people from rest of the word. All these developments had made economic and financial recovery in the country very difficult.

Another reason which highlights the economic and environmental impact of the floods is that it had mainly affected the fertile tracts of Indus River basin which are considered as the growth pole of the economy. Around 65 per cent area of Pakistan is covered by the basin and vast stretches of fertile tracts, covering Punjab, Sindh and Balochistan. These tracts also happen to be the main producing areas of agricultural products and industrial development. This region is also characterised by large concentration of population and development of telecommunication networks. Many urban centres of Pakistan including its capital territory also lie in this region. On account of the floods, many parts of the basin remained under water for many weeks which had brought to halt all human activities. Industrial production had stopped and movement of the people including all means of communication also came to a standstill. Around 20 million people including thousands of workers were displaced by the floods. A large number of them had lost their work and many could not come back to their work. Thus, those sectors of the economy, production areas and activities which should have supported the country during the crisis were themselves victims of the floods. For the reversal of the flood impact and the recovery of the economy further investment was needed, which had further deepened the crisis. Foreign assistance in this regard was also very low and untimely.

Finally, the floods happened when the country was facing many other pressing challenges. That period was marked by the internal instability and continuing and intensified security challenges to the country which had been continuing since 2001. In addition, the country also faced multiple adverse shocks of commodity and oil prices and the fallout of the global financial crisis. Due to these problems, the country had already lost billions of dollars and economic growth rate was very low. Inflationary pressures caused by the floods had brought pressure on the interest rate, with much of the credit flowing in the government sector, private credit remained weak. With development resources pre-empted by un-anticipated expenditures on flood relief and power and petroleum subsidies, fiscal discipline required the government to reduce its public investment to a low level for many years. Accordingly, the overall investment in the year was also below its level over the previous years. Therefore, in that period of crisis, losses of more than US $ 10 billion due to the floods proved to be disastrous to the development of the economy.

Unlike other losses, some environmental losses (including faunal, floral, pedological, natural processes) are irreversible also. There was no exact estimation available for these losses, but, some information and research show that physical losses to environment have degraded ecological services which may take many years to recover. Environmental impact of the floods was most visible in the production patterns of most *rabi* (winter) crops. The floods had happened just before the harvesting of key crops and on the onset of the wheat planting season which normally starts in September/October. Many crops including rice, *jowar*, barley, gram, sesamum, cotton and tobacco, etc. had registered a decline in their cultivation area due to the floods. In case of Pakistan, even this temporal decline in the total area under food crops was very significant, because, for many years, overall performance of the agriculture sector had been far below the satisfactory level. As a typical natural process, floods provide sustenance also which is indicated by the increased yields of wheat, sugarcane, maize, cotton, etc. One of the irreversible losses of the floods may be the loss of over 1.2 million head of livestock (excluding poultry). Thousands of wild animals and birds (many of them declared endangered) also died during the floods. Loss of fertile soils especially in hilly areas may take hundreds of years to develop cultivable a layer. Recurring floods and the absence of effective intervention measures for the restoration of environmental and ecological services may further add to the already fragile environment.

The climate, drainage system and the topography of the land make Pakistan a natural floods-prone area. Pakistan also lies in a seismic belt and experiences earthquakes of varying magnitude. Its long coastline also increases the risks of potential tsunamis and cyclones. Consequently, many ravaging floods have hit this country in the last century. Irrational human intervention with the environment has further added to the possibilities of the occurrence of floods and loss of lives and properties. Therefore, floods have been occurring in Pakistan more frequently in recent years. In the year 2011 and 2012 also, vast areas of the country experienced devastating floods that killed hundreds of people and damaged properties worth millions of dollars. With the long history of disasters due to ravaging floods, now it has become imperative that serious attention be paid towards their management and prevention. However, in spite of huge losses and tragedies, the governments and the concerned agencies have not evolved any long-term strategy for the prevention and management of floods. These agencies still largely follow 'response centric' approach and policies and not much has been achieved to reach the stage of 'preparedness and prevention' to minimise the impact of floods.

One major question after the floods was to analyse whether these floods were predictable, and if so, why was the government and concerned agencies not prepared to deal with the flooding and its after effects? First of all policy makers and planners have to recognise that Pakistan is one of the countries which are prone to natural calamities, therefore, ad hocism and 'response centric' approach has to be abandoned for effective flood control. There are technologies available which help in the prediction of rainfall with greater accuracy and precision. There is evidence that in case of the 2010 floods also, it was possible to predict the occurrence of heavy rainfall a week in advance of the floods. But, the threat and magnitude levels of the floods were not correctly estimated. Desperate measures like breaking levee, releasing of excess water from dams, diversion and channelisation of water had also flooded many areas and resulted in economic and environmental losses. There was no effective and readymade plan for the management of the floods and the safety of the people. Government agencies in Pakistan also lack trained manpower, modern technology, financial and other resources.

There are many lessons that can be learnt from the experience of the 2010 floods. All concerned agencies need to be update with knowledge and information about the hazard, risk assessment and management and need to work by establishing coordination among them. They need to develop plans which do not allow the calamity of this magnitude to happen again. All physical, financial, technological and administrative measures should be taken to prevent normal flooding from becoming a hazard. In medium and long term plans, priority should be given to environmental management and awareness. The existing risk analysis apparatus of the country is weak and spreads across multiple agencies; the forecasting and warning system for floods is also outdated and needs technical updating. There is also a need to identify vulnerable locations and high risk regions to put up better flood defenses and also relocate residents permanently from those regions.

Dependency on foreign aid has only corrupted and corroded the country's institutions. In fact import of technology and cooperation in the field of disaster management will certainly help Pakistan in coping with flood losses. In this direction, beginning of the damage and need assessment (DNA) by the government in collaboration with the WB and ADB is a welcome step in rehabilitation of people and development of resources. Though, it is also true that due to climate change and other causes, sudden floods have taken place in other parts of the world also. But, the extent of human, environmental and economic losses recorded in Pakistan are incomparable. One of the reasons for this may be the corruption and mismanagement of flood waters which the Supreme Court of Pakistan had to take note of and cautioned the government in 2010.[81] Recurring floods have created a situation with long-term environmental, economic and political consequences. The floods not only obliterated the GDP growth achieved in that year but also weakened the resilience of the environment. All this could have been saved and utilised for the welfare of the society.

Pakistan needs to do all it can to stop such weather disasters becoming catastrophes. The government has to assess the safety of every barrage and dam for their capacity-building and optimum utilisation. Most of these structures are weak and do not have capacity to safely pass the floods of very high magnitude. The country urgently needs to step up efforts to increase the resilience of infrastructure, economy and communities including better emergency warning and evacuation systems. To prevent future catastrophic flood disasters, the government should improve forecasting especially medium range forecasting from existing 2-3 days to

81. M.A. Khan, F.K. Khan, A.W. Kazi, K.Z. Ahmed, Op. Cit.

10 days. If necessary, it should take the help of neighbouring countries in improving their capabilities.

There is urgent need to carry out both macro and micro-level watershed management studies for developing anatomy of every flood. Flood plain mapping and zoning all along the Indus River and its tributaries for restricting and prohibiting permanent settlements in high and medium flood risk areas needs to be carried out with an urgency. Massive deforestation which has taken place in KP, POK and GB is also one of the causes of the severity of floods and deposition of silt and sand in rivers, water channels and reservoirs. Afforestation with local species of trees and plants should be carried out especially in those areas which are affected by hill torrents (fast moving water from hills) and suffer massive soil erosion. The challenges are enormous and the country cannot stop the occurrence of floods but its policies and preparedness may certainly minimise the enormous environmental and economic loss which the country has been suffering from.

Figure 1: Administrative Divisions of Pakistan

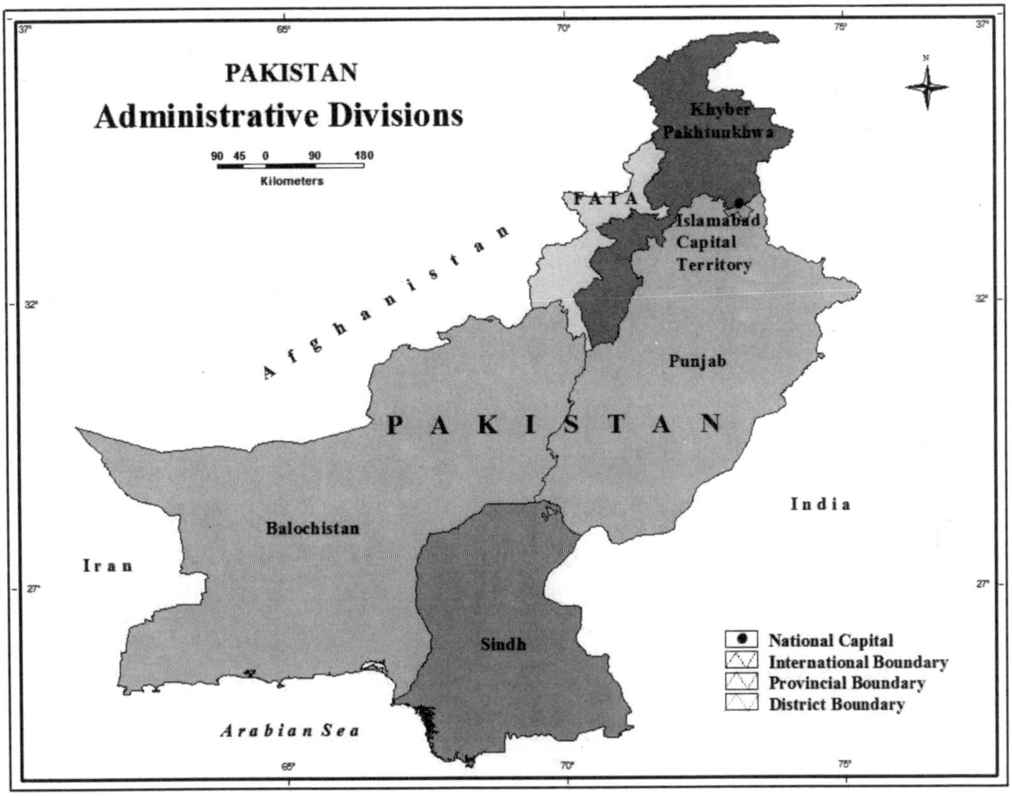

Source: Based on information available at United Nations, Cartographic Section, Department of Field Support, http://www.un.org/Depts/Cartographic/map/profile/pakistan.pdf (Accessed on 12 July 2013).

Figure 2: Physiographic Divisions of Pakistan

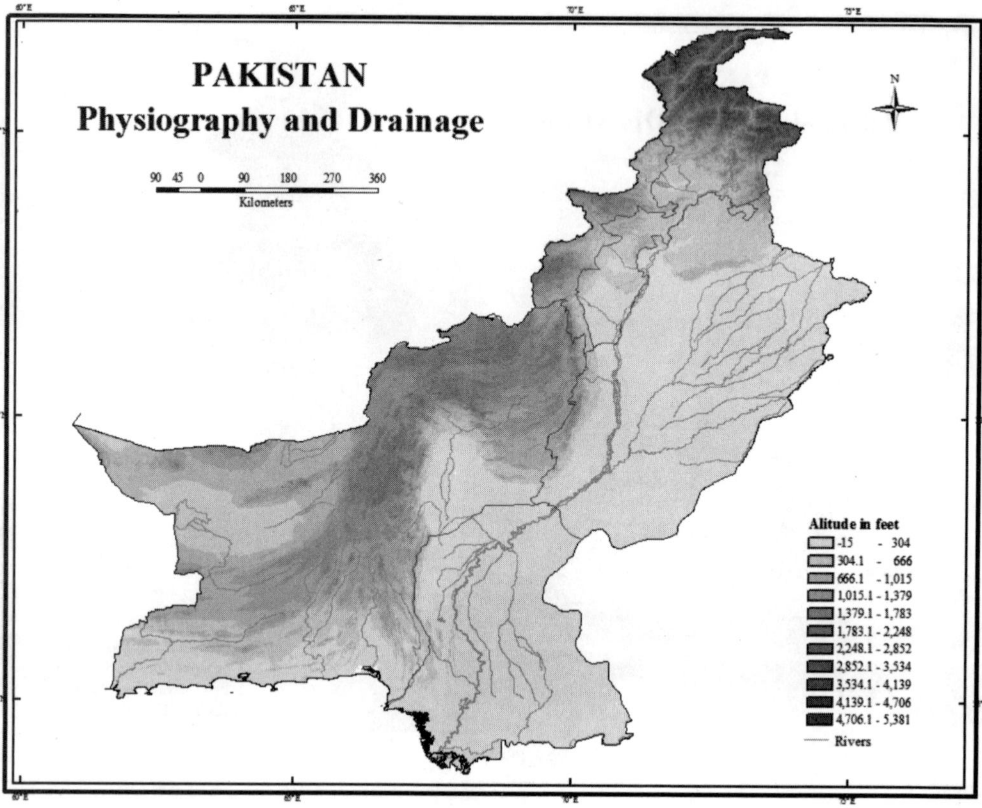

Source: Based on data and information available at Humanitarian Response Pakistan, http://pakresponse.info/MapDataCenter/GISData.aspx (Accessed on 22 October 2013).

Figure 3: Distribution of Average Annual Rainfall in Pakistan

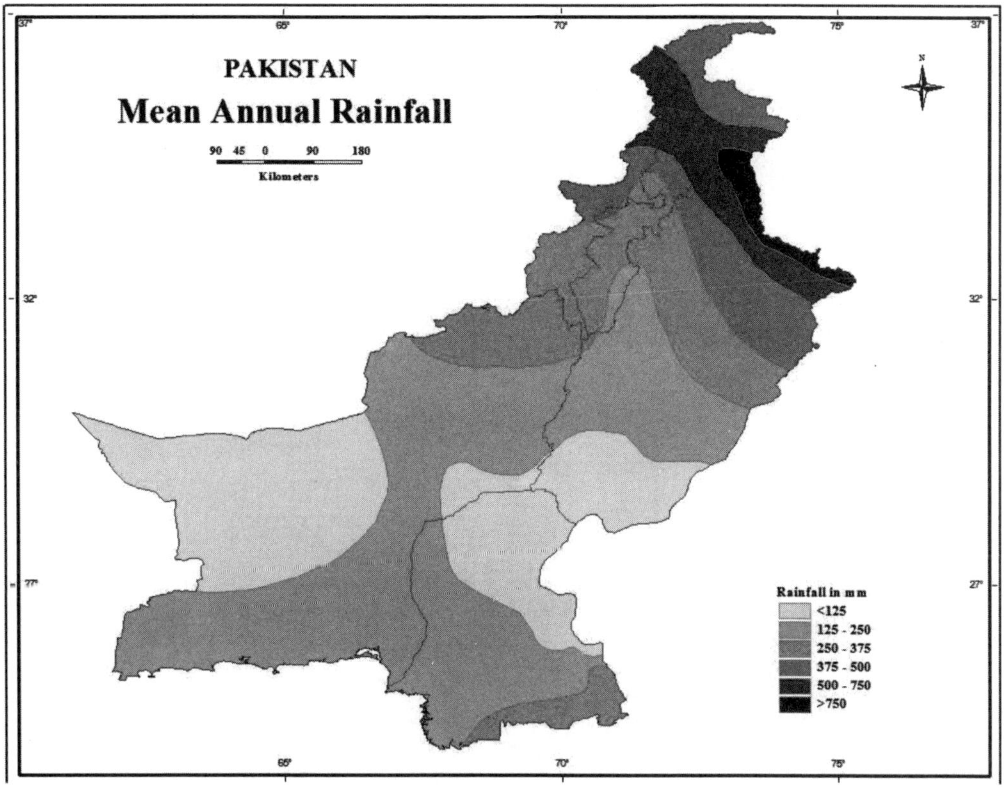

Source: Based on data and information available at Humanitarian Response Pakistan, http://pakresponse.info/MapDataCenter/GISData.aspx (Accessed on 22 July 2013).

Figure 4: Flood Routing Model of Pakistan

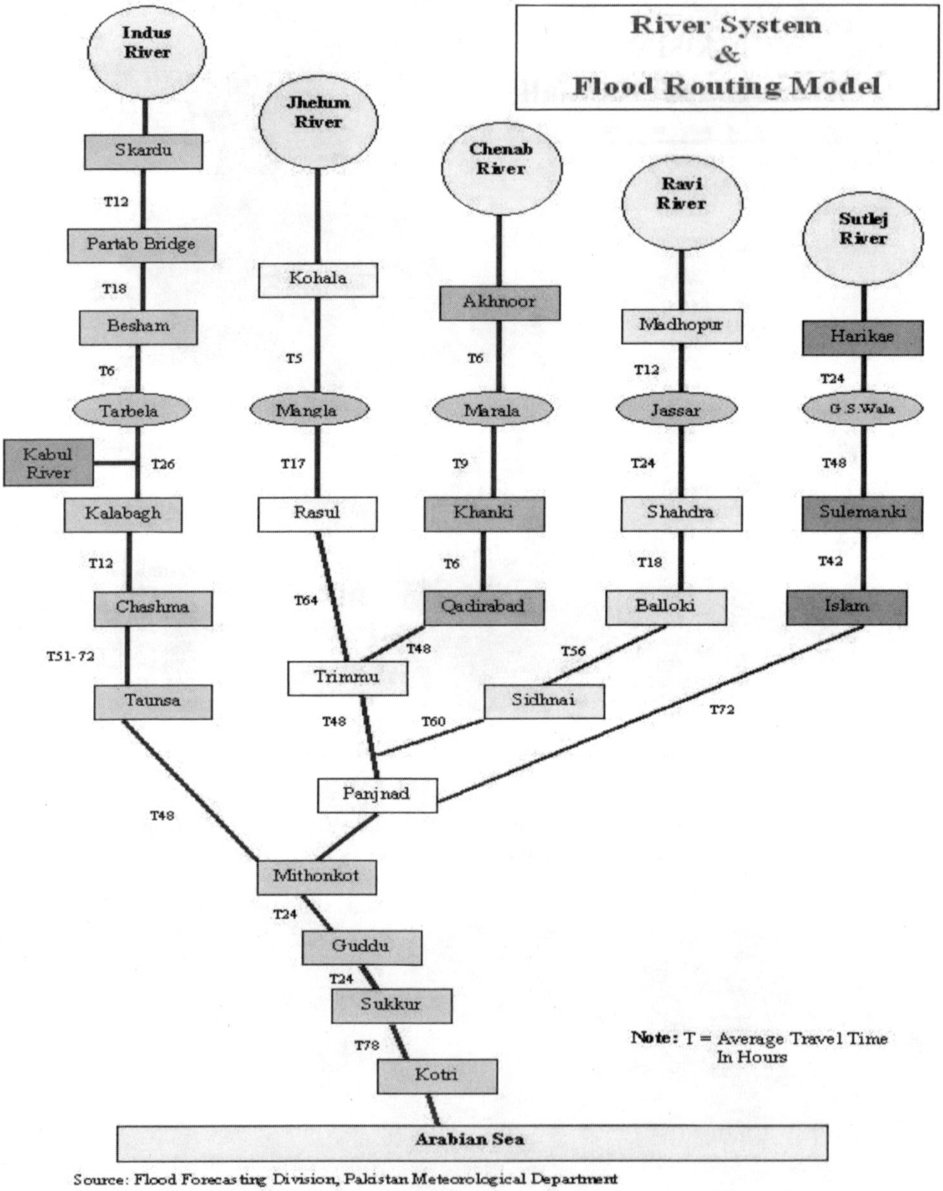

Source: Pakistan Meteorological Department, Government of Pakistan, "Flood Routing Model," Available at http://www.pmd.gov.pk/FFD/index_files/frm.htm (Accessed on 11 July 2013).

Figure 5: Indus Basin Irrigation System

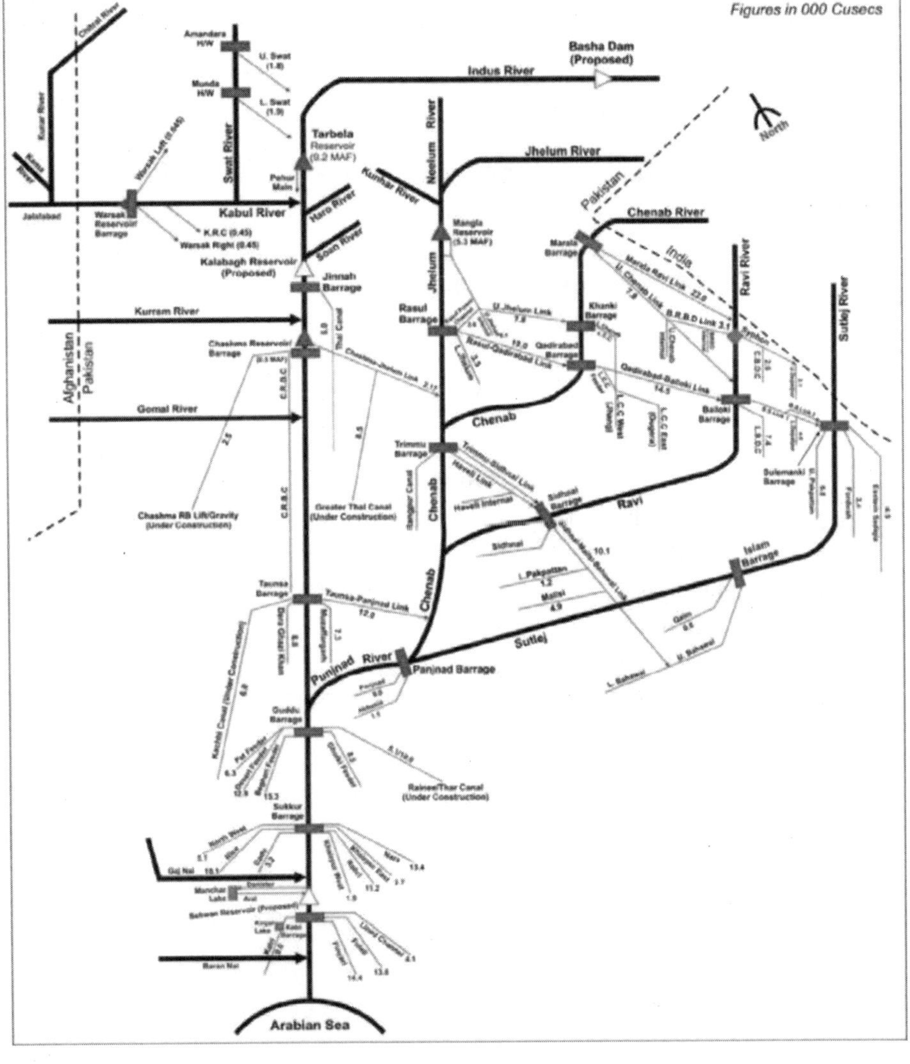

Source: Project Management and Policy Implementation Unit (PMPIU), *Handbook on Water Statistics of Pakistan* (Islamabad: Ministry of Water and Power, Government of Pakistan, 2011), p. 65.

Figure 6: Causes and Types of Floods in Pakistan

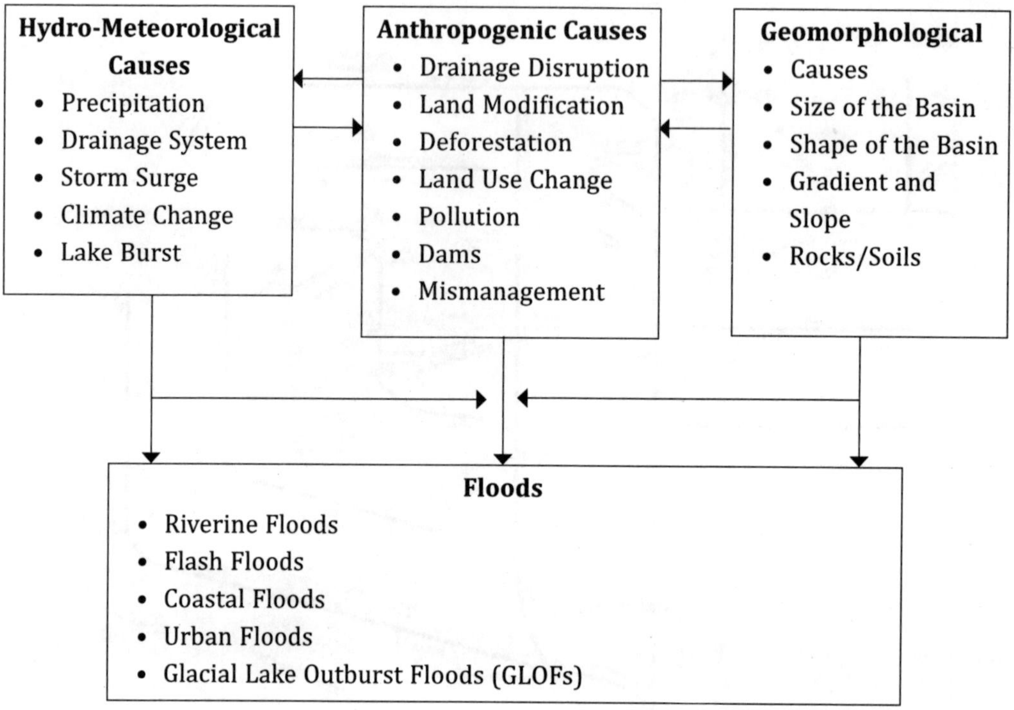

Figure 7: Extent of Flooded Area in Pakistan in 2010

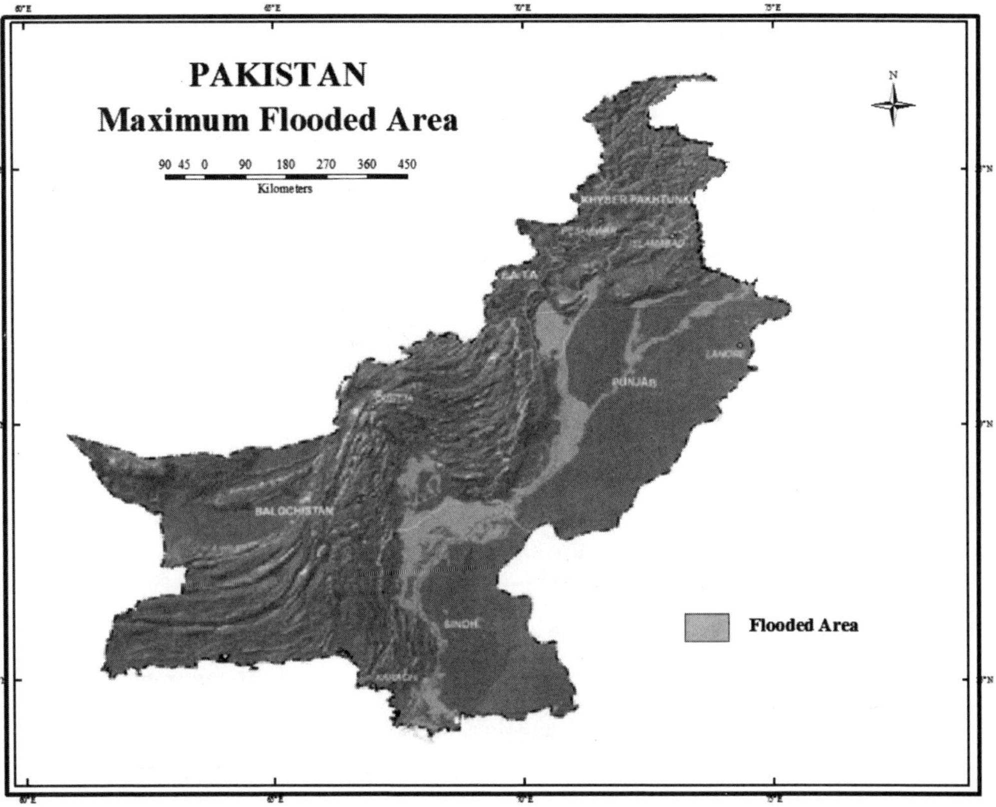

Source: World Bank, Asian Development Bank & Government of Pakistan, *Pakistan Floods 2010: Preliminary Damage and Needs Assessment* (Islamabad: 2010), p. 12. Available at https://www.gfdrr.org/sites/gfdrr.org/files/publication/Pakistan_DNA.pdf (Accessed on 10 July 2013).

Figure 8: Flood Affected Districts of Pakistan

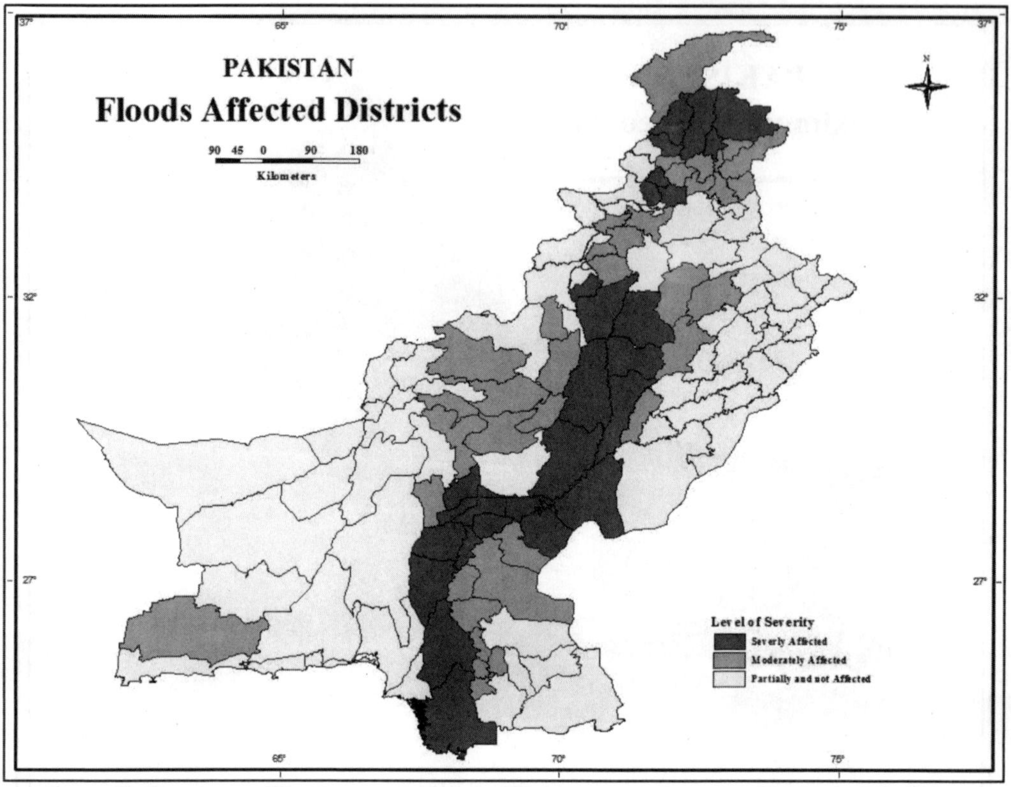

Source: National Disaster Management Authority (NDMA), Government of Pakistan, "List of Flood affected district 2010," Available at http://www.ndma.gov.pk/Documents/flood_2010/Map_Flood_Affected_Districts_2010.pdf (Accessed on 22 October 2013).

Figure 9: Environmental Impact of the 2010 Floods in Pakistan

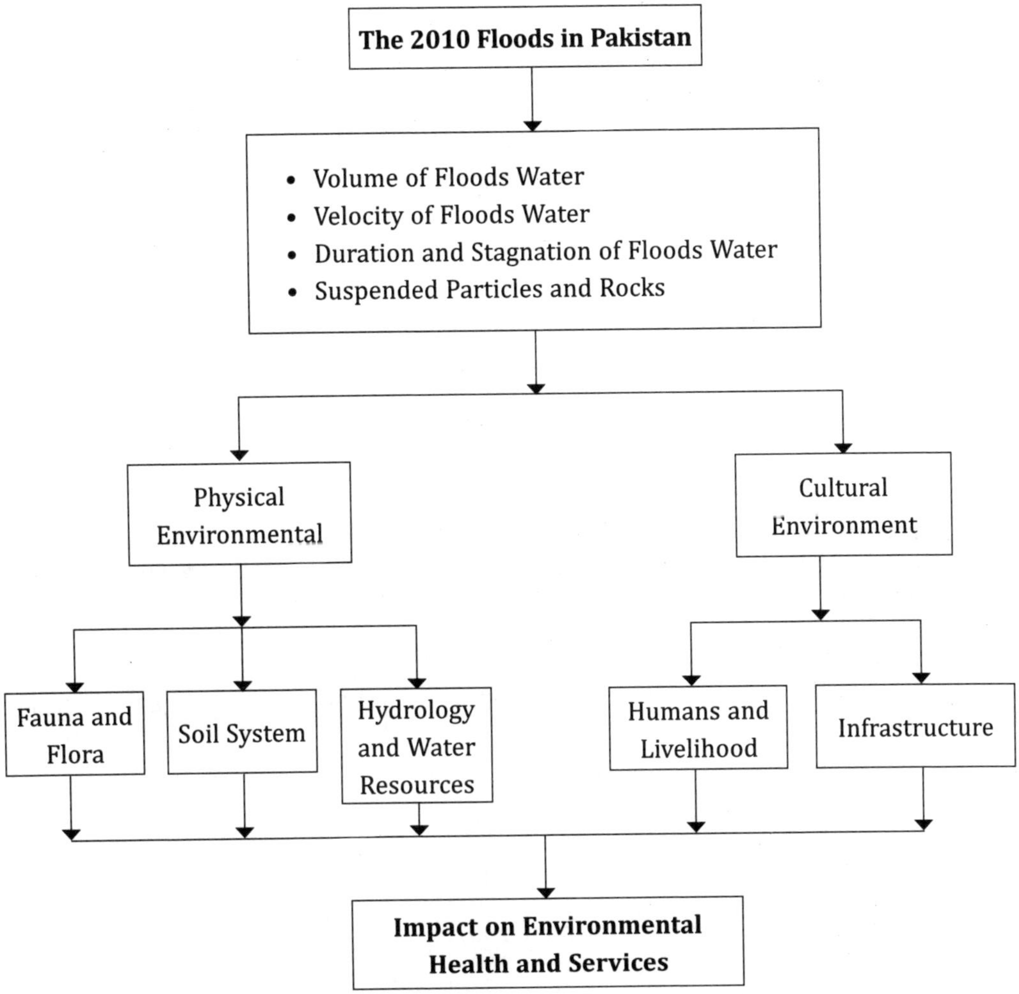

Table 1: Capacity of Major Reservoirs

(Million acre feet MAF)

Reservoirs Running Length in Feet	Original			Capacity in (2011)			Loss		
	Gross	Live	Dead	Gross	Live	Dead	Gross	Live	Dead
Tarbela (1,378-1,550)	11.62	7.72	3.90	7.73	6.63	1.10	3.89	1.09	2.80
Mangla (1,040-1,210)	6.41	5.87	0.54	5.12	5.02	0.10	1.29	0.85	0.44
Chashma (637-649)	0.87	0.72	0.15	0.32	0.26	0.06	0.55	0.45	0.09
Total	18.90	14.31	4.59	13.18	11.91	1.27	5.72	2.40	3.32

Source: Water and Power Development Authority (WAPDA), *Annual Reports 2010-11* (Lahore: Ministry of Water & Power, Government of Pakistan, 2011), p. 66. Available at http://www.wapda.gov.pk/pdf/Annual%20Report%202010-11.pdf (Accessed on 15 September 2013).

Table 2: Historical Flood Damages in Pakistan

Year	Property Damaged (Million US $)	Lives Lost	Villages Affected	Flooded Area Km^2	Year	Property Damaged (Million US $)	Lives Lost	Villages Affected	Flooded Area Km^2
1950	488.05	2,190	10,000	17,920	1992	3,010.00	1,008	13,208	38,758
1955	378.40	679	6,945	20,480	1994	842.80	431	1,622	5,568
1956	318.20	160	11,609	74,406	1995	376.25	591	6,852	16,686
1957	301.00	83	4,498	16,003	1998	NR	47	161	NA
1959	234.35	88	3,902	10,424	2001	450.00	219	50	NA
1973	5,134.20	474	9,719	41,472	2003	5,175.00	484	4,376	NA
1975	683.70	126	8,628	34,931	2004	15.00	85	47	NA
1976	3,485.15	425	9,150	81,920	2005	NR	59	1,931	NA
1977	337.55	848	2,185	4,657	2006	NR	523	2,477	NA
1978	2,227.4	393	9,199	30,597	2007	327.00	586	6,498	NA
1981	298.85	82	2,071	4,191	2008	103.00	NA	–	NA
1983	135.45	39	643	1,882	2009	NR	NA	–	NA
1984	75.25	42	251	1,093	2010	10,056.00	1,985	17,553	75,633*
1988	857.85	508	1,000	6,144	Total	35,310.45	12,875	1,34,575	5,67,132

Source: A.O.N. Benfield, *Impact Forecasting*: *Pakistan Flood Event Recap Report*, 31 August 2010, (London: Aon Corporation, 2010), p. 10. Available at http://www.aon.com/attachments/reinsurance/201008_pakistan_flood.pdf (Accessed on 14 August 2013). Also see World Conference on Disaster Reduction (WCDR), *A Review of Disaster Management Policies and Systems in Pakistan* (Islamabad, 2005), p. 5 and Himayatullah Khan and Abuturab Khan, "Natural Hazards and Disaster Management in Pakistan," *African Journal of Agricultural Research*, Vol. 7, No. 7, October 2008, p. 8.

NR= Not Reported, NA= Not Available.

* Different estimates are available with different government agencies and research organisations.

Table 3: Rainfall during the Four Day Wet Spell of 27 to 30 July 2010

S.N.	City	Rainfall in (mm)	Province	S.N.	City	Rainfall in (mm)	Province
1.	Risalpur	468.0*	KP	12.	Muzaffarabad	292.0	POK
2.	Cherat	384.0*	KP	13.	Pattan	242.0	POK
3.	Saidu Sharif	338.0*	KP	14.	Islamabad	394.0	Capital Territory
4.	Peshawar	226.1*	KP	15.	Murree	373.0	Punjab
5.	Lower Dir	297.0	KP	16.	Kamra	308.0	Punjab
6.	Kohat	127.3	KP	17.	Lahore	288.0	Punjab
7.	Balakot	208.7	KP	18.	Mianwali	271.0*	Punjab
8.	Upper Dir	309.0	KP	19.	Jhelum	269.0	Punjab
9.	D. I. Khan	83.3	KP	20.	Sialkot	255.0	Punjab
10.	G. Dopatta	346.0	POK	21.	Gujranwala	222.0	Punjab
11.	Rawalakot	297.0	POK	22.	Rawalpindi	219.0	Punjab

Source: Federal Flood Commission, Government of Pakistan, *Annual Flood Report 2010* (Islamabad: Ministry of Water and Power, Government of Pakistan, 2010), p. 27. Available at http://www.ffc.gov.pk/download/flood/archieve/Annual.report2010.pdf (Accessed on 22 July 2013).

* Indicates New Record.

Table 4: Historic Maximum vs 2010 Maximum Peak Discharge of Major Rivers of Pakistan

S.N.	River	Barrages/ Head-Works/ Bridges	Designed Capacity	Historic Maximum Peak (Cusecs)		Maximum-2010 Peak (Cusecs)	
				Flood	Date	Flood	Date
1.	Indus	Tarbela	15,00,000	5,10,000	31-7-89	8,33,000	30-7-10
		Kalabagh	9,50,000	9,50,000	14-7-42	9,37,453	30-7-10
		Chashma	9,50,000	7,86,600	3-8-76	10,36,673	01-8-10
		Taunsa	11,00,000	7,88,646	22-7-58	9,59,991	02-8-10
		Guddu	12,00,000	11,99,672	15-8-76	11,48,738**	8&9-8-10
		Sukkur	15,00,000*	11,66,574	15-8-76	11,31,000#	9&11-8-10
		Kotri	8,75,000	9,81,000	14-8-56	9,64,900	27-8-10
2.	Jhelum	Mangla	10,60,000	9,33,000	10-9-92	3,44,400	30-7-10
		Rasul	8,50,000	9,32,000	10-9-92	2,63,800	30-7-10
3.	Kabul	Warsak	5,40,000	1,50,680	8-7-78	1,52,710	30-7-10
		Nowshera	–	–	–	2,49,100^	10-8-10
4.	Chenab	Marala	11,00,000	11,00,000	26-8-57	3,14,378	06-8-10
		Qadirabad	8,07,000	9,48,530	11-9-92	3,29,483	07-8-10
		Trimmu	6,45,000	9,43,225	8-7-59	3,28,926	11-8-10
		Panjnad	7,00,000	8,02,516	17-8-73	3,10,000	13-8-10
5.	Ravi	Balloki	2,25,000	3,89,845	28-9-88	69,900	23-8-10
		Sidhnai	1,50,000	3,30,210	2-10-88	27,600	28-7-10
6.	Sutlej	Sulemanki	3,25,000	5,97,000	8-10-55	58,300	03-9-10

Source: Federal Flood Commission, Government of Pakistan, *Annual Flood Report 2010*, p. 28.

* Existing design capacity as reported by Provincial Irrigation Department (PID), Sindh is 9,00,000 cusecs.

** Does not include flood flows passed through breach of Left Marginal Bund (LMB) of Guddu Barrage.

Does not include flood flows passed through Tori Bund reach u/s Sukkur Barrage.

^ The gauges were submerged at this discharge, it is estimated that a flood more than 4,50,000 cusecs passed through this point.

Table 5: Flood Affected Area in Pakistan, 2010

S.N.	Provinces	Number of Affected Districts	Total Area in Km^2	Total Affected Area in Km^2	Total Affected Area in Percentage
1.	POK	2	12,431	272	2.19
2.	Baluchistan	8	3,47,190	8,147	2.35
3.	FATA	4	27,220	182	0.67
4.	KP	16	74,521	9,169	12.30
5.	Punjab	32	2,05,345	29,463	14.35
6.	Sindh	18	1,40,914	28,036	19.90
7.	GB	6	68,879	364	0.53
	Pakistan	86	7,96,095	75,633	9.50

Source: SUPARCO & FAO, *Pakistan Floods Rains 2010,* Op. cit., p. 17.

Table 6: Environment-Damage, Reconstruction and Restoration Costs

USD millions*

S.N.	Description	R1	R2
A.	**Institutional Frameworks, Planning, and Capacity Building to Reduce the Risk of Floods**	**26.30**	
1.	Storm Water Drainage Master Plan for Urban Areas	8.40	–
2.	Land Use Plans and Building Regulations in Urban Areas	2.80	–
3.	Monitoring and Evaluation and Information Databases.	5.20	–
B.	**Strengthening Legal and Institutional Frameworks**	**5.60**	–
C.	**Restoration of Natural Systems in the Indus Watershed**	**117.56**	–
1.	Restoration of Riparian/Non-Riparian Forests and Wildlife Resources	11.67	–
2.	Forest Restoration	44.12	1,326.47
3.	Riparian Vegetation Restoration.	51.89	280.96
4.	Wetland Restoration	4.00	108.00
5.	Mangrove Restoration	5.88	149.41
D.	**Burden on Environmental Health and Proposed Responses**	**64.59**	–
1.	Disease Vectors from Stagnant Water	7.49	–
2.	Waste Handling		–
3.	Marginal Landfills Over a Period of Six Months	14.80	–
4.	Hazardous Waste	30.00	–
5.	Medical Waste	0.40	–
6.	Debris Disposal	11.90	–
E.	**Additional Studies**	**0.40**	–
	Total	**208.85**	**1,864.84**

Source: WB, ADB & Government of Pakistan, Op. Cit., pp. 63-66.

R1= Medium to Long Term Requirements, R2= Medium to Long Term Requirements (US $ Million)*

* Converted from Pakistani currency at the rate of 85 PKR = 1 US $ (As adopted by the World Bank, Asian Development Bank & Government of Pakistan for the estimation and calculation of damage and need assessment in the country in the wake of the 2010 floods. Monthly average of the exchange rates for the months of July to October 2010 also comes at 84.93 US $. For details see State Bank of Pakistan, *Statistical Bulletin,* December 2010 (Islamabad: Economic Analysis Department, 2011), p. 7).

Table 7: Estimated Damage and Reconstruction Costs by Province and Area

USD millions*

Province/Region	Direct Damage*	Indirect Losses*	Total Damage*	Reconstructions Cost*		
				Option 1	Option 2	Option 3
POK	64	22	86	155	163	188
Balochistan	494	126	620	321	404	684
FATA	48	26	74	89	93	112
GB	43	6	49	78	81	118
KP	796	376	1,172	1,247	1,293	2,116
Punjab	1,803	777	2,580	1,100	1,269	1,384
Sindh	2,980	1,400	4,380	2,681	2,987	3,173
Federal/Cross Cutting Sectors	268	827	1,095	1,128	1,128	1,140
National Total	6,496	3,560	10,056	6,799	7,418	8,915

Source: WB, ADB & Government of Pakistan, Op. Cit., pp. 19 & 49.

* Converted from Pakistani currency at the rate of 1 US $ = 85 PKR
Option 1.25 Building as before; Option 2.25 Restoration to flood resistant; Option 3.25 Building back better

Table 8: Estimates of Total Damage and Reconstruction Costs by Sector

USD millions*

Sectors	Direct Damage*	Indirect Losses*	Total Damage*	Reconstructions Options*		
				Option 1	Option 2	Option 3
1. Social Infrastructure						
Housing	1,080	508	1,588	1,483	1,690	2,206
Health	19	31	50	49	49	49
Education	259	52	311	505	505	505
Subtotal	1,358	591	1,949	2,037	2,244	2,759
2. Physical Infrastructure						
Irrigation & Flood Management	278	–	278	427	427	982
Transport & Communications	735	593	1,328	2,356	2,356	2,356
Water Supply & Sanitation	37	72	109	74	74	94
Energy	155	154	309	106	106	106
Subtotal	1,206	819	2,025	2,973	2,973	3,539
3. Economic Sector						
Agriculture, Livestock and Fisheries	3,712	1,332	5,045	257	670	1,049
Private Sector & Industries	170	112	282	102	102	129
Financial Sector	1	673	674	463	463	463
Social Protection & Livelihood	–	–	–	683	683	683
Subtotal	3,884	2,116	6,000	1,505	1,918	2,323
4. Cross-Cutting Sectors						
Governance	37	33	70	58	58	58
Environment	12	–	12	209	209	209
Disaster Risk Management	–	–	–	27	27	27
Subtotal	49	33	82	293	293	293
Total	6,496	3,560	10,056	6,799	7,418	8,915
Percentage of 2009-10 GDP	3.8	2.1	5.8	3.9	4.3	5.2

Source: WB, ADB & Government of Pakistan, Op. Cit., p. 18.

* Converted from Pakistani currency at the rate of 85 PKR= 1 US $

Table 9: Housing (Consolidated Damage Details)

Province/ Region	No. of Affected *Pucca* Housing Unit			No. of Affected *Katcha* Housing Unit			Total House Damaged in Number			% of Pre-Floods Stock
	CD	PD	Total	CD	PD	Total	CD	PD	Total	
POK	541	2,316	2,857	1,090	2,896	3,986	1,631	5,212	6,843	1.0
Balo.	800	1,500	2,300	73,724	3,696	77,420	74,524	5,196	79,720	14.0
FATA	0	0	0	1,241	4,178	5,419	1,241	4,178	5,419	1.0
GB	0	0	0	3,157	0	3,157	3,157	0	3,157	2.0
KP	4,107	8,282	12,389	90,605	1,54,300	2,44,905	94,712	1,62,582	2,57,294	9.0
Punjab	4,050	8,127	12,177	1,23,572	2,40,024	3,63,596	1,27,622	2,48,151	3,75,773	9.0
Sindh	56,353	70,441	1,26,794	5,54,067	1,99,118	7,53,185	6,10,420	2,69,559	8,79,978	24.0
Total	65,851	90,666	1,56,517	8,47,456	6,04,212	14,51,668	9,13,307	6,94,878	16,08,184	13.0

Source: WB, ADB & Government of Pakistan, Op. Cit., p. 89.

CD = Completely Destroyed, PD = Partially Damaged

Table 10: Housing (Losses, Recovery and Reconstruction Assessment)

USD million*

Province/ Region	Value of Housing Stock (Direct Damage)*			Total Indirect Losses*	Total Damages and Losses*	Total Repair and Reconstruction Cost*		
	CD	PD	Total			Option 1 Base Case	Option 2 Flood Resistant	Option 3 Multi-Hazard Resistant
POK	3.2	4.6	7.8	1.8	9.6	4.99	4.99	9.79
Balochistan	65.0	2.7	67.7	29.1	96.8	90.73	90.73	309.92
FATA	1.1	1.4	2.5	1.0	3.5	3.92	3.92	7.57
GB	3.9	0.0	3.9	1.2	5.1	3.72	3.72	13.00
KP	96.6	67.2	163.8	61.7	225.5	207.06	209.86	488.43
Punjab	125.7	97.9	223.6	98.8	322.4	296.12	365.35	365.36
Sindh	499.8	111.3	611.2	314.3	925.5	876.7	1,011.74	1,011.74
Total	795.3	285.2	1,080.5	507.9	1,588.4	1,483.24	1,690.29	2,205.79

Source: WB, ADB & Government of Pakistan, Op. Cit., p. 91 and p. 94.

CD = Completely Destroyed, PD = Partially Damaged

* USD million converted from Pakistani currency at the rate of 85 PKR= 1 USD

Table 11: Health Facilities: An Overview of Damage and Reconstruction Needs

Province/ Region	Total Health Facilities of all Categories	Number of Damage Health Facilities			Affected Facilities in Percentage	Reconstruction Cost in USD Million*		
		CD	PD	Total		CD	PD	Total
POK	616	6	33	39	6.30	0.53	1.21	1.74
Balochistan	2,075	26	19	45	2.10	0.93	0.68	1.61
FATA	364	0	30	30	8.24	0	0.80	0.80
GB	731	2	1	3	0.41	0.02	0.0004	0.03
KP	1,739	40	150	190	10.90	4.67	7.64	12.31
Punjab	2,891	9	48	57	2.00	1.24	2.29	3.53
Sindh	1,305	103	48	151	11.65	14.57	2.15	16.72
Total	9,721	186	329	515	5.29	21.96	14.77	36.74

Source: WB, ADB & Government of Pakistan, Op. Cit., p. 99 and p. 102.

CD = Completely Destroyed, PD = Partially Damaged
* USD million converted from Pakistani currency at the rate of 85 PKR= 1 USD

Table 12: Education (Damage and Reconstruction Needs)

USD million*

Province/ Region	No. of Institutions with Physical Damage		Damage and Loss*			Reconstruction Needs*		
	Schools	College/ Technical and Vocational Institutions	Damage	Loss	Total	Short Term	Long Term	Total
POK	194	4	9.21	0.70	9.91	0.72	13.73	14.45
Balochistan	557	0	7.16	1.97	9.13	2.54	12.87	15.41
FATA	176	0	4.26	0.62	4.88	0.78	6.56	7.34
GB	79	2	3.67	0.29	3.96	0.4	5.96	6.40
KP	870	30	30.41	3.23	33.64	4.14	48.72	52.90
Punjab	2,817	8	75.10	17.63	92.73	21.3	118.35	139.70
Sindh	5,655	0	129.57	27.55	157.12	33.78	234.93	268.71
Total	10,348	44	259.37	51.97	311.34	63.65	441.13	504.80

Source: WB, ADB & Government of Pakistan, Op. Cit., p. 107 and p. 109

Short-term = 6-12 months, Long-term = 12-36 months
* Converted from Pakistani currency at the rate of 85 PKR= 1 USD

Table 13: Irrigation and Flood Management (Damage and Needs Assessment)

USD million*

Province/ WAPDA	Damage and Loss			Year 1	Year 1-2		Total
	Direct Damage	Indirect Loss[1]	Total	Reconstruction	Reconstruction	Building - Back Safer	
POK	0.16	-	0.16	0.13	0.12	11.12	11.37
Balochistan	29.60	-	29.60	15.59	29.96	0.00	45.55
FATA	3.00	-	3.00	1.78	2.84	12.94	17.56
GB	1.62	-	1.62	0.56	1.93	24.71	27.2
KP	68.35	-	68.35	33.44	71.55	495.35	600.34
Punjab	33.09	-	33.09	17.28	33.64	0.00	50.92
Sindh	136.92	-	136.92	84.26	126.39	0.00	210.65
FFC	0.00	-	0.00	0.00	0.00	2.00	2
PMD	0.00	-	0.00	0.00	0.00	9.24	9.24
WAPDA	4.89	-	4.89	2.35	5.18	0.00	7.53
Total	277.65	-	277.65	155.39	271.60	555.35	982.36

Source: WB, ADB & Government of Pakistan, Op. Cit., p. 123 and p. 126.

1 The indirect losses mainly relate to agriculture and livelihoods and are mentioned in the relevant sector (Table 19 & 20)

* Converted from Pakistani currency at the rate of 85 PKR= 1 USD

Table 14: Transport and Communication (Damage to Road Infrastructure)

Length in kilometres

Province/ Region	No. of Motorways/ National Highways	No. of Provincial Highways	Length of District Roads		Length of Municipal Roads/ Urban Roads	Total*
			Paved	Unpaved		
POK	35	0	1,910	1,570	61	3,576
Balochistan	5	367	816	11.5	878	2,077.5
FATA	0	294	497	466	0	1,257
GB	33	0	90	260	0	383
KP	402	259	3,510	1,974	366	6,511
Punjab	53	281	2,206	0	279	2,819
Sindh	265	1,925	4,060	2,217	0	8,467
Total	793	3,126	13,089	6,498.5	1,584	25,090.5

Source: WB, ADB & Government of Pakistan, Op. Cit., p. 129.

* Includes both completely damaged and partially damaged roads.

Table 15: Transport and Communication (Damage/Loss and Reconstruction Needs)

USD million*

Province/ Region	Damage and Loss Figures*			Reconstruction Needs Assessment Summary*				
	Direct Damage	Indirect Losses	Total	Rehabilitation and Reconstruction Cost	Social Safeguards (6%)	Project Management and Capacity Building (8%)	Escalation (12%)	Total
Roads:								
POK	23.58	11.02	34.60	82.73	4.96	6.62	9.93	104.25
Balochistan	16.74	21.16	37.91	56.98	3.42	4.55	6.84	71.79
FATA	19.02	4.36	23.39	51.02	3.06	4.08	6.12	64.28
GB	13.80	0.99	14.79	44.56	2.67	3.56	5.35	56.15
KP	222.04	115.54	337.58	547.48	32.85	43.8	65.69	689.82
Punjab	44.82	134.14	178.96	234.49	14.07	18.76	28.14	295.47
Sindh	316.05	289.09	605.14	627.52	37.65	50.2	75.31	790.67
Subtotal	656.06[a]	576.32	1,232.38	1,644.76	98.68	131.58	197.38	2,072.4
Railways:								
Balochistan	8.73	3.32	12.05	38.35	2.31	3.07	4.6	48.33
KP	8.89	0.74	9.64	39.16	2.35	3.13	4.69	49.34
Punjab	10.05	8.05	18.09	44.01	2.64	3.52	5.28	55.45
Sindh	15.56	4.75	20.32	68.12	4.08	5.45	8.18	85.82
Subtotal	43.24	16.86	60.09	189.65	11.38	15.18	22.75	238.95
Civil Aviation	0.66	0.00	0.66	-	-	-	-	-
Telecommunication	35.24	0.00	35.24	-	-	-	-	-
Total	735.19	593.18	1,328.36	1,834.41	110.07	146.75	220.13	2,356.26[b]

Source: WB, ADB & Government of Pakistan, Op. Cit., p. 131 and p. 133.

* Converted from Pakistani currency at the rate of 85 PKR= 1 USD

a. Also includes rehabilitation and reconstruction cost of USD 263.67 million for motorways/national highways

b Also includes telecommunication and civil aviation needs of US $ 44.9 million which is a private sector. Excluding this, the public sector needs amounts to US $ 2311 million.

Table 16: Water Supply and Sanitation

USD million*

Province/ Region	Damage and Loss*			Recovery and Reconstruction Needs Assessment*				Total
				Option- 1	Option- 2, Recommended Additional Investment			
	Direct Damage	Indirect Loss	Total	A**	B	C	D	
POK	2.93	0.29	3.22	5.73	0.24	0.47	0.07	6.51
Balochistan	2.34	3.51	5.85	4.66	0.29	0.65	0.53	6.13
FATA	0.49	0.24	0.73	0.98	0.06	0.18	0.04	1.26
GB	0.48	0.14	0.62	0.96	0.06	0.18	0.04	1.24
KP	8.48	11.32	19.80	17.06	0.47	1.18	1.86	20.57
Punjab	5.06	16.53	21.59	10.19	0.59	1.47	2.94	15.19
Sindh	17.79	39.88	57.67	34.45	0.65	1.76	6.18	43.04
Total	37.58	71.91	109.48	74.02	2.35	5.88	11.65	93.90

Source: WB, ADB & Government of Pakistan, Op. Cit., p. 138 and p. 141.

A= Reconstruction and Rehabilitation/ Repair Costs, B= Management System, Training and Disaster Preparedness, C= Infrastructure Services Planning and Energy Audits, D= Policy and Communication

* 85 PKR= 1 USD, **Includes US $ 2.93 million for priority system cleaning, de-clogging and disinfection

Table 17: Energy Sector (Physical Damage Details)

S.N.	Assets Type	Completely Destroyed	Partially Destroyed
A	**Power Sector**		
1.	Grid Stations (No.)	1	31
2.	Transmission Lines (Km.)	65	96
3.	Distribution Lines (Km.)	2,799	434
4.	Distribution Transformers (No.)	5,299	340
5.	Customer Connections (No.)	1,06,299	27,421
6.	Equipments (US $ Million)	7.18	–
7.	Hydro Power Plants[a] (No.)	–	91
8.	Thermal Plants	–	1
B	**Petroleum Sector**		
1.	Oil Refineries (No.)	–	1
2.	Site Offices (No.)	–	2
3.	Oil Pipeline (Km.)	–	274
4.	Oil Depots (No.)	–	3
5.	Petrol Stations[b] (No.)	10	125
6.	Gas Distribution[c] (Locations)	–	310
7.	LPG Facilities	–	1
8.	CNG Stations	5	10
9.	Oil/Gas Fields (Sites)	–	15

Source: WB, ADB & Government of Pakistan, Op. Cit., pp. 145-146.

a Includes 60 micro hydro power plants in GB and 15 in FATA, and 6 plants in POK

b Indicative assessment. Some of these stations have already been restored.

c Major locations include pipeline segments, stations, rural and urban towns/districts, camps etc. as reported by gas companies.

Table 18: Energy Damage/Loss and Reconstruction Assessment

USD million*

Entity	Damage and Loss*			Recovery and Reconstruction Needs Assessment*		
	Direct Damage	Indirect Loss	Total	Reconstruction Rehabilitation and Repair Cost	Capacity Building	Total
Generation	53.07	57.27	110.34	-	-	-
Transmission	0.96	0	0.96	-	-	-
Distribution	35.95	7.27	43.22	-	-	-
Total Power	89.98	64.54	154.52	63.79	10	73.79
Oil Downstream	9.58	37.94	47.52	32.54**	-	32.54**
Gas Downstream	50.62	22.15	72.78	-	-	-
Upstream Oil & Gas	4.91	29.67	34.58	-	-	-
Total Oil and Gas	65.11	89.76	154.88	-	-	-
National	155.09	154.30	309.40	96.33	10	106.33

Source: WB, ADB & Government of Pakistan, Op. Cit., p. 147 and p. 149.

* Converted from Pakistani currency at the rate of 85 PKR– 1 USD

** Petroleum only

Table 19: Damage of Agriculture and Livestock

S.N.	Descriptions	POK	Baloc-histan	FATA	GB	KP	Punjab	Sindh	National
1.	Crop Area Damaged*	33.1	132.5	7.22	7.9	121.5	746.9	1,043.5	2,092.64
2.	Large Animals**	0.3	139.6	6.2	1.3	72.4	2.3	93.7	315.61
3.	Small Animals (Includes Sheep, Goat)**	0.3	1,036.7	8.4	10.8	67.8	2.5	81.9	1,208.38
4.	Poultry Perished**	11.7	625.5	101.2	12.9	621.3	2,012.0	6,895.1	10,279.73
5.	Fishery/Ponds Lost***	n/a	n/a	-	n/a	0.15	3.75	0.58	4.48
6.	Water Courses Damaged****	657	47	n/a	960	1,790	2,598	6,990	13,042
7.	Household Stocks of Food, Seed & Feed***	0.88	18.71	n/a	0.22	79.10	421.23	123.39	643.53
8.	Agriculture Machinery, Tools***	n/a	0.68	n/a	n/a	1.00	53.40	1.33	56.41
9.	Government Buildings, Infrastructure Facilities***	n/a	0.18	n/a	n/a	2.91	17.22	0.01	20.32

Source: WB, ADB & Government of Pakistan, Op. Cit., p. 153.

Large animals include cattle, buffaloes, camel, horse and donkey.
Small animal includes sheep and goat.
Fisheries/ponds lost in FATA included in estimates for KP.
* In thousand hectares
** In thousand
*** Amount in (US $ million) converted from Pakistani currency at the rate of 85 PKR= 1 USD
**** In numbers

Table 20: Estimates of Direct and Indirect Loss of Agriculture and Livestock

USD million*

Province	Livestock			Crops			Fisheries/ Pond Damage	Total
	Direct Damage	Indirect Damage	Sub Total	Direct Damage	Indirect Damage	Sub- Total		
POK	0.19	0	0.19	17.29	6.82	24.11	n/a	24.3
Balochistan	144.52	21.68	166.2	219.48	40.85	260.33	n/a	426.53
FATA	6.72	3.74	10.46	10.83	15.33	26.16	0	36.62
GB	1.98	0	1.98	17.17	2.81	19.98	n/a	21.96
KP	62.09	51.37	113.46	188.61	93.46	282.07	0.15	395.68
Punjab	24.74	61.08	85.82	1,355.79	392.69	1,748.48	3.75	1,838.05
Sindh	86.99	101.43	188.42	1,571.43	541.19	2,112.62	0.57	2,301.61
Total	327.24	239.29	566.53	3,380.60	1,093.15	4,473.75	4.48	5,044.76

Source: WB, ADB & Government of Pakistan, Op. Cit., p. 154.

Fisheries/ponds lost in FATA included in estimates for Khyber Pakhtunkhwa.
Note: Total livestock lost due to flood represents about one per cent of total national stock and value terms it is about 11 per cent of total sector loss.

* Converted from Pakistani currency at the rate of 85 PKR= 1 USD

Table 21: Agriculture and Livestock (Costs for Recovery and Reconstruction)

USD million*

Key Intervention Area	Cost Options		
Key Intervention Area 1: Restoring Normalcy and Rebuilding Agriculture and Rural Livelihood	**Low Cost Option**	**Medium Cost Option**	**High Cost Option**
A. Crops Seed/Fertilizers/Land Preparation/Tools and Implements for *Rabi* 2010-11 and For *Kharif* 2011	161.00	453.00	754.00
B. Livestock Restocking, Feed/Medicine, Animal Shelters	29.00	128.00	194.00
C. Fisheries Repair of Fish Hatcheries and Stocking of Ponds	2.70	2.70	2.70
D. On-Farm Water Management Repair of Damaged Infrastructure (Water Courses, Tube Wells Etc.)	44.06	66.00	77.00
Sub-Total	237.40	649.7	1,028.64
Key Intervention Area 2: Strengthening Key Government Policies Related to Management of Flood and Riverine Areas	20.00	20.00	20.00
Total Programme Cost	257.4	669.7	1,048.635

Source: WB, ADB & Government of Pakistan, Op. Cit., p. 157.

* Converted from Pakistani currency at the rate of 85 PKR= 1 USD

Table 22: Agriculture and Livestock (Estimated Costs for Key Intervention Area 1)

USD million*

Province/ Region	Low Compensation Scenario	Medium Compensation Scenario - Preferred Option	High Compensation Scenario
POK	5.17	13.36	21.57
Balochistan	49.07	132.60	189.94
FATA	1.41	4.69	7.50
GB	2.57	5.69	8.35
KP	23.26	67.34	106.90
Punjab	59.67	159.64	262.01
Sindh	96.29	266.45	432.37
Total	237.44	649.77	1,028.64

Source: WB, ADB & Government of Pakistan, Op. Cit., p. 158.

* Converted from Pakistani currency at the rate of 85 PKR= 1 USD

Table 23: Private Sector & Industries (Damage and Reconstruction Cost)

USD million*

Province/ Area	Damage (No. of Enterprises)**			Damage and Loss			Reconstruction Costs	
	Industrial Units	Shops and Hotels	Mines	Direct Damage	Indirect Loss	Total	Option 1	Option 2
POK	-	494	-	0.52	0.12	0.64	1.21	1.30
Balochistan	-	6,519	-	8.42	1.96	10.38	5.10	6.60
FATA	-	217	-	0.21	0.07	0.28	1.11	1.10
GB	-	36	-	0.02	0.01	0.03	1.04	1.00
KP	89	17,702	236	34.95	20.27	55.22	20.90	26.30
Punjab	41	40,322	-	41.78	35.02	76.80	26.90	34.20
Sindh	16	54,283	-	84.25	53.94	138.19	45.30	58.00
Total	146	1,19,572	236	170.15	111.39	281.54	102.00	129.00

Source: WB, ADB & Government of Pakistan, Op. Cit., pp. 163-166.

* Converted from Pakistani currency at the rate of 85 PKR= 1 USD

** Includes both completely and partially damaged units

Table 24: Financial Sector (Damage, Loss and Recovery Estimates)

USD million*

Sectors	Physical Damage			Loan Losses			TO	Recovery Estimates		
	PU	PR	TO	PU	PR	TO		PU	PR	TO
Banks	0.48	0.41	0.89	438.26	177.75	616.01	616.9	328.96	94.64	423.6
MF Sector (MFIs & MFBs)	-	0.4	0.4	-	25.36	25.36	25.76	-	39.44	39.44
Leasing	-	-	-	-	15.68	15.68	15.68	-	-	-
Insurance	-	-	-	-	15.16	15.16	15.16	-	-	-
Total	0.48	0.81	1.29	438.26	233.95	672.21	673.5	328.96	134.08	463.04

Source: WB, ADB & Government of Pakistan, Op. Cit., p. 170 and p. 172.

* Converted from Pakistani currency at the rate of 85 PKR= 1 USD
PU= Public, PR= Private, TO= Total, MFIs= Micro-finance Institutions, MFBs= Micro-finance Banks

Table 25: Social Protection and Livelihoods (Estimates of Severely Affected Households)

Province/ Area	Total Affected Population	Percentage of Total Affected Population	Total Household Affected	Severely Affected Household		Cash Grants for Six Months (in US $ Million)*	
				Specification 1	Specification 2	Specification 1	Specification 2
POK	8,01,905	4.20	1,23,370	38,727	43,621	13.6	15.8
Balochistan	9,02,639	4.73	1,32,741	1,02,868	1,02,259	36.1	36.3
FATA	2,43,546	1.28	26,188	11,463	12,314	4.0	4.4
GB	1,68,676	0.88	25,950	9,790	10,724	3.4	3.9
KP	28,80,339	15.10	3,60,042	2,78,410	2,83,131	97.7	100.3
Punjab	73,29,358	38.42	11,10,509	5,57,793	6,07,836	195.7	215.6
Sindh	67,49,915	35.38	11,24,986	8,63,609	8,65,840	303.0	306.9
Total	1,90,76,378	100.00	29,03,786	18,62,660	19,25,725	654.0	683.0

Source: WB, ADB & Government of Pakistan, Op. Cit., p. 177 and 179.

* Converted from Pakistani currency at the rate of 85 PKR= 1 USD.
Cash grants at the rate of PKR 5000/month (US $ 58.82) for a period of six months.

Table 26: Governance Infrastructure (Damage, Recovery and Needs Assessment)

USD million*

Province/ Region	Damage and Losses			Recovery and Needs Assessment		
	Direct Damage	Indirect Losses	Total	Reconstruction and Rehabilitation and Repair Cost	Capacity Building	Total
POK	1.02	0.01	1.03	1.22	0.37	1.59
Balochistan	0.50	0.83	1.32	0.60	0.10	0.70
FATA	0.31	0.00	0.31	0.37	0.11	0.48
GB	0.28	0.62	0.90	0.34	0.18	0.52
KP	11.51	8.14	19.65	13.81	4.14	17.96
Punjab	1.42	9.84	11.27	1.71	0.51	2.22
Sindh	21.92	13.92	35.84	26.30	7.89	34.19
Total	36.95	33.35	70.31	44.34	13.30	57.65

Source: WB, ADB & Government of Pakistan, Op. Cit., p. 117 and p. 119.

* Converted from Pakistani currency at the rate of 85 PKR= 1 USD

Table 27: Cost of Environmental and Natural Resource Damages in Pakistan, 2006

S.N.	Types of Environmental Damages	Value of Damage* US $ Billion	Amount of Damage According to the Value of PKR Against US $ in 2010** US $ Billion
1.	Water Supply, Sanitation and Hygiene	1.86	2.62
2.	Agriculture Soil Degradation	1.16	1.63
3.	Indoor Pollution	1.11	1.56
4.	Urban Air Pollution	1.08	1.52
5.	Lead Exposure	0.75	1.05
6.	Rangeland Degradation and Deforestation	0.09	0.14
	Total	6.05	8.52

Source: World Bank, *Pakistan Strategic Country Environmental Assessment, Vol. 1* (Islamabad: South Asia Environment and Social Development Unit, South Asia Region, 2006), p. 6. Available an http://siteresources.worldbank.org/SOUTHASIAEXT/Resources/Publications/448813-1188777211460/pakceavolume1.pdf (Accessed on 11 December 2013).

* Converted from Pakistani Rupees at the of US $1.00 = 60.32 PKR (August 18, 2006)

** In August 2010, the conversion rate was US $1.00 = 85 PKR. According to this figure inflation rate has been calculated to be 40.91 per cent. Figures for 2010 have been achieved by inflating base year value i.e. 2006.

Table 28: Area, Production and Yield of Important Crops

FISCAL YEAR	W	R	BJ	J	M	BR	TF	G	S	R & M	SE	C	T
	Area in thousand hectares												
2009-10	9,132	2,883	476	248	935	84	13,758	1,067	943	178	80	3,106	56
2010-11	8,901	2,365	548	229	974	77	13,094	1,054	988	203	78	2,689	51
2011-12P	8,666	2,571	458	214	1,083	75	13,067	1,055	1,046	213	76	2,835	47
	Production in thousand tons												
2009-10	23,311	6,883	293	154	3,261	71	33,973	562	49,373	151	33.4	2,196	119
2010-11	25,214	4,823	346	141	3,707	71	34,302	496	55,309	176	31.0	1,949	103
2011-12P	23,517	6,160	304	137	4,271	70	34,459	291	58,038	186	30.2	2,312	94
	Yield in kg/ha												
2009-10	2,553	2,387	616	621	3,487		2,469	527	52,357	848	418	707	2,125
2010-11	2,833	2,039	631	616	3,806		2,620	471	55,981	867	397	724	2,020
2011-12P	2,714	2,396	664	640	3,944		2,637	276	55,486	873	397	815	2,000

Source: Ministry of Finance, Government of Pakistan, *Economic Survey of Pakistan 2011-2012* (Islamabad: Economic Adviser's Wing, Finance Division, 2012), pp. 40-42. Also see Pakistan Bureau of Statistics, *Agricultural Statistics of Pakistan 2010-11* (Islamabad: Statistics Division, 2011), pp. 2-105.

P= Provisional (July-March), W= Wheat, R= Rice, BJ= *Bajra*, J= *Jowar*, M= Maize, BR= Barley, TF= Total Food-grains, G= Gram, S= Sugarcane, R&M= Rapeseed and Mustard, SE= Sesamum, C= Cotton, T= Tobacco

Table 29: Average Number of Livestock per Household before and after the Flood

S.N.	Livestock	GB			KP			Punjab			Sindh			Nation		
		BF	AF	PC	BF	AF	PC	BF	AF	PC	BF	AF	PC	BF	AF	PC
1.	Cows	2.4	1.9	24	0.7	0.4	39	2.2	1.8	20	3.2	1.1	66	2.2	1.4	38
2.	Buffaloes	0.4	0.4	7	0.5	0.4	31	1.3	0.9	25	2.7	1.2	56	1.5	0.9	40
3.	Sheep/Goats	10.3	5.2	49	0.5	0.4	26	3.0	2.4	21	4.1	1.5	65	3.1	1.9	39
4.	Poultry	9.0	2.0	78	3.3	1.0	71	4.9	1.6	68	3.9	0.7	83	4.5	1.3	72
5.	Horses	0.0	0.0	NA	0.1	0.0	NA	0.1	0.0	NA	0.1	0.0	NA	0.1	0.0	NA
6.	Oxen	0.2	0.1	NA	0.1	0.1	NA	0.2	0.1	NA	0.0	0.1	NA	0.1	0.1	NA
7.	Donkeys/Mules	0.1	0.1	NA	0.0	0.0	NA	0.2	0.2	NA	0.3	0.1	NA	0.2	0.1	NA
8.	Camels	0.0	0.0	NA	0.0	0.0	NA	0.1	0.3	NA	0.1	0.0	NA	0.1	0.1	NA

Source: World Food Programme (WFP), *Pakistan Flood Impact Assessment: September 2010* (Islamabad: Country Office Pakistan, 2010), p. 12.

BF = Before Floods, AF= After Floods, PC= Percentage Changes in Minus, NA=Not Available

Table 30: Inflation Trends (December 2009 to December 2010)

Figures in per cent

Months and Year	CPI						Core Inflation				WPI		SPI	
	General		Food		Non-Food		NFNE*		Trimmed					
	YoY	MoM	YoY	MoM	YoY	MoM	YoY	MoM	YoY	MoM	YoY	MoM	YoY	MoM
Dec-09	10.5	-0.5	10.9	-1.7	10.2	0.6	10.7	0.7	10.4	0.6	15.0	0.2	11.9	0.3
Jan-10	13.7	2.4	15.5	2.0	12.2	2.8	10.3	0.7	12.7	1.3	19.6	4.2	17.8	3.2
Feb-10	13.0	0.4	14.9	0.1	11.5	0.6	10.1	0.8	12.4	0.7	19.3	0.4	17.2	0.9
Mar-10	12.9	1.3	14.5	1.8	11.6	0.8	9.9	0.8	12.7	0.8	21.8	2.5	17.6	1.1
Apr-10	13.3	1.7	14.5	2.0	12.2	1.5	10.6	1.7	12.7	1.1	22.0	1.8	17.4	1.0
May-10	13.1	0.1	14.8	0.0	11.7	0.1	10.3	0.6	12.5	0.4	21.2	0.9	17.4	0.8
Jun-10	12.7	0.6	14.5	0.7	11.2	0.6	10.4	0.7	11.7	0.7	17.6	-0.6	16.5	0.4
Jul-10	12.3	1.2	12.8	1.5	12.0	1.0	10.3	0.5	12.0	0.7	18.7	1.7	14.9	1.8
Aug-10	13.2	2.5	15.6	5.1	11.2	0.3	9.8	0.4	12.5	0.7	19.2	2.6	16.2	2.6
Sep-10	15.7	2.7	21.2	5.3	11.0	0.3	9.4	0.4	12.8	0.9	21.5	2.1	19.1	3.5
Oct-10	15.3	0.6	20.1	0.1	11.3	1.1	9.3	0.7	12.8	1.0	23.8	3.1	20.9	1.7
Nov-10	15.5	1.5	20.5	2.2	11.1	0.9	9.5	1.0	13.4	1.2	24.7	3.5	22.5	3.3
Dec-10	15.5	-0.5	20.4	-1.9	11.4	0.8	9.5	0.7	13.6	0.7	25.7	1.1	21.5	-0.5

Source: State Bank of Pakistan, *Inflation Monitor: July 2010* (Islamabad: Economic Analysis Department, 2010a), pp. 1 & 31. Available at http://www.sbp.org.pk/publications/Inflation_Monitor/2010/Dec/IM_Dec_2010.pdf (Accesses on 12 November 2013).

* NFNE is Non-Food Non-Energy Inflation; ** SPI for all income groups combined.
WPI=Wholesale Price Index; SPI=Sensitive Price Indicator; YoY=Year on Year; MoM=Month on Month

Table 31: Domestic Commodity Prices

(Prices in Pakistani rupees)

S.N.	Items	Units	Prices in July 2010	Prices in September 2010	Percentage Change
1.	Wheat	Kg.	23.9	25.5	6.69
2.	Wheat Flour	Kg.	27.2	29.0	6.62
3.	Rice Basmati (Broken)	Kg.	44.7	46.6	4.25
4.	*Moong* Pulse (Washed)	Kg.	115.6	138.4	19.72
5.	*Mash* Pulse (Washed)	Kg.	166.1	172.3	3.73
6.	Gram Pulse (Washed)	Kg.	57.8	71.5	23.70
7.	Beef	Kg.	193.5	207.8	7.39
8.	Mutton	Kg.	366.7	388.2	5.86
9.	Eggs Hen (Farm)	Dozen	59.6	74.4	24.83
10.	Sugar	Kg.	62.8	81.3	29.46
11.	*Gur*	Kg.	72.6	87.4	20.39
12.	Milk Fresh	Per litre	45.9	46.9	2.18
13.	Vegetable *Ghee* (Loose)	Kg.	116.2	131.0	12.74
14.	Mustard Oil	Kg.	135.9	142.6	4.93
15.	Potatoes	Kg.	25.6	35.7	39.45
16.	Onions	Kg.	22.9	40.1	75.11
17.	Tomatoes	Kg.	25.6	56.2	119.53
18.	Bananas	Dozen	48.3	48.8	1.04
19.	Salt (Powdered)	Kg.	6.9	7.0	1.45
20	Red Chillies (Powdered)	Kg.	176.2	186.1	5.62
21.	Garlic	Kg.	163.5	211.1	29.11
22.	Kerosene	Per litre	77.0	77.1	0.13
23.	Firewood	40 kg.	312.8	323.3	3.36
24.	Washing Soap	1 cake	13.4	13.8	2.99
25.	Bath Soap (Lifebuoy)	1 cake	22.0	24.0	9.10
26.	Chicken (Farm)	Kg.	125.2	145.3	16.05
27.	L.P.G. (Cylinder 11 kg.)	Each	935.2	1,108.3	18.51

Source: State Bank of Pakistan, *Inflation Monitor: July 2010* (Islamabad: Economic Analysis Department, 2010), p. 20. Also see State Bank of Pakistan, *Inflation Monitor: September 2010* (Islamabad: Economic Analysis Department, 2010), p. 21.

Table 32: Increases in Prices after Floods
(Prices in August Compared with that of July 2010)

Figures in percentage

S.N.	Province	KP+				Sindh*	
	District/ Commodity	Kohistan	Lower Dir	Manshra	Swat	Kamber	Hyderabad
1.	Wheat Flour	82	33	10	26	7	6
2.	Broken Basmati Rice	87		7	33	-10	10
3.	IRRI6-Rice	–	25	6	38	12	19
4.	Split Peas	22	18	22	31	–	–
5.	Edible Oil	–	11	22	17	–	–
6.	*Pakwan Ghee*	9	16	17	18	–	–
7.	Dalda *Ghee*	–	9	5	–	–	–
8.	Sugar	43	16	8	14	13	12
9.	Onion	–	–	–	–	41	25
10.	Chicken	–	–	–	–	65	69
11.	Beef	–	–	–	–	9	25
12.	Mutton	–	–	–	–	8	13

Source: WFP, *Pakistan Flood Impact Assessment: September 2010*, p. 9.

\+ Based on data collected by the Federal Bureau of Statistics (KP) for the WFP for July and August 2010.

* WFP data for August 2010 compared with Federal Bureau of Statistics data for July 2010.

Table 33: Tax Collection by Federal Board of Revenue in Pakistan 2010

(PKR Billion)

S.N.	Months	Direct	Indirect Taxes				Total Tax
			Sales	Excise	Customs	Total	Collection*
1.	April	46.0	46.2	10.8	14.0	71.0	116.9
2.	May	36.7	47.9	11.7	14.0	73.6	110.3
3.	June[P]	103.7	52.1	14.3	21.7	88.2	191.8
4.	July	18.1	40.8	7.3	11.0	59.0	77.1
5.	August	28.5	54.2	10.3	13.0	77.4	105.9
6.	September	51.6	41.3	9.2	14.2	64.8	116.4

Source: State Bank of Pakistan, *Statistical Bulletin,* December 2010 (Islamabad: Economic Analysis Department, 2011), p. 231.

P Provisional

* Total may not match due to the rounding of figures.